Cambridge Elements ≡

Elements in Environmental Humanities
edited by
Louise Westling
University of Oregon
Serenella Iovino
University of North Carolina at Chapel Hill
Timo Maran
University of Tartu

SLIME

An Elemental Imaginary

Simon C. Estok
Sungkyunkwan University

CAMBRIDGE
UNIVERSITY PRESS

Shaftesbury Road, Cambridge CB2 8EA, United Kingdom

One Liberty Plaza, 20th Floor, New York, NY 10006, USA

477 Williamstown Road, Port Melbourne, VIC 3207, Australia

314–321, 3rd Floor, Plot 3, Splendor Forum, Jasola District Centre, New Delhi – 110025, India

103 Penang Road, #05–06/07, Visioncrest Commercial, Singapore 238467

Cambridge University Press is part of Cambridge University Press & Assessment, a department of the University of Cambridge.

We share the University's mission to contribute to society through the pursuit of education, learning and research at the highest international levels of excellence.

www.cambridge.org
Information on this title: www.cambridge.org/9781009550703

DOI: 10.1017/9781009550680

First published 2024

A catalogue record for this publication is available from the British Library

ISBN 978-1-009-55070-3 Hardback
ISBN 978-1-009-55069-7 Paperback
ISSN 2632-3125 (online)
ISSN 2632-3117 (print)

Slime

An Elemental Imaginary

Elements in Environmental Humanities

DOI: 10.1017/9781009550680
First published online: December 2024

Simon C. Estok
Sungkyunkwan University
Author for correspondence: Simon C. Estok, estok@skku.edu

Abstract: Slime has always stirred the imagination and evoked strong responses. It is as central to life and growth as to death, degeneration, and rot. Slime heals and cures; it also infects and kills. Slime titillates and terrifies. It fascinates children and is the horror in stories and the disgusting in fridges. Slime is part of good sex. Slime is also worryingly on the rise in the warming oceans. Engaging with slime is becoming more urgent because of its proliferation both in the seas and in our imaginations. Inextricable from racism, homophobia, sexism, and ecophobia, slime is the least theorized element and is indeed traditionally not even included among the elements. Things need to change. Addressing growing climate issues and honestly confronting matters associated with them depend to a very large degree on theorizing and thus understanding how people have thought and continue to think about slime.

Keywords: slime, ecogothic, horror, ecophobia, zombies

ISBNs: 9781009550703 (HB), 9781009550697 (PB), 9781009550680 (OC)
ISSNs: 2632-3125 (online), 2632-3117 (print)

Contents

Introduction: Theorizing Slime

Slime is an important element because it defines the very parameters of life, from the primordial slime through which life began to the rot and slime to which life decomposes. Slime is important because it titillates and terrifies. For children, it is a curiosity; for horror film buffs, it is essential to the affect that the films produce; for lovers, it is a lubricant. Slime is important because of the responses it evokes and the imaginations it stirs. Slime is on the rise. As the high end of food chains in our global seas disappears, jellyfish proliferate, and there is an increasing presence of oceanic slime. With the increase of oceanic slime, the environmental implications of how we imagine and represent slime are also increasingly important. Slime is an element that often defies intellectual and material control. "Like the supernatural," as Middlebury professor Dan Brayton has explained, "it mediates the overlap between nature and culture at the margins of the unknown" (Brayton 2015, 88). In so doing, it evokes the imagination at various points on an unusually broad spectrum and travels through some very well-known sites: unmistakably gendered, raced, and classed,[1] slime is connected with ideologies and commerce, with values and ethics, and with self and other. It connects and disconnects us, to each other and to the world. Understanding the growing importance of cultural imaginations of slime will help to mediate the environmental struggles we face by furthering understanding of the roots and effects of responses to slime. Slime's ubiquity is palpable, and its dearth in discussions within the Environmental Humanities, pronounced.

The elemental turn in the Environmental Humanities revisits old concerns with new perspectives, and expanding elemental discussions to include slime and recognizing that slime is gendered, raced, and classed sheds light on our art, ourselves, and our current environmental crises. In their introduction to the *Zeitschrift für Anglistik und Amerikanistik* special issue on "Elemental Agency," Moritz Ingwersen and Timo Müller note that in "resituating the human in its conditioning environments, an elemental analysis also resituates agency itself by tracing the distribution of agency across the supposedly inert material world" (Ingwersen and Müller 2022, 12). To bring slime into these discussions is important because the elemental agency of slime is one that we imbue with volition: slime is sometimes the benign mold that can recreate "the motorway network of the United

---

[1] Early modern misogyny, often centering on the idea of women as "the leaky vessel" (see Section 2.1), is part of a broader historical spectrum of sexism that genders slime – including slime-mouthed mother aliens in blockbuster films, Jean-Paul Sartre's theorizing of slime, and monstrosities such as Donald Trump suggesting that the reason behind what he imagined as hostile questioning from reporter Megyn Kelly was that she had "blood coming out of her whatever" (see Rucker 2015). I discuss these issues, as well as race and class, directly in Sections 2.2, 2.3, and 2.4 – and elsewhere throughout.

States" or find "the shortest path to the exit" at IKEA (Sheldrake 2020, 15);[2] at other times, it is the apogee of an imagined hostile agential elementality, one that infects and kills. For the most part, slime has not been a part of happy imaginings of nature. It is necessary, therefore, to understand our resistances to slime, for "as repellent as we find slime today, it has played a significant part in the history of science as the presumed link between [...] inanimate matter and life on Earth" (Wedlich 2021, 105). Recent and forthcoming work on slime's "part in the history of science" finds expression in historian Christopher Pastore's research. In a kind of preview to a book he is working on entitled *A Thousand, Thousand Slimy Things: A Natural History of the Sea from the Bottom Up*, Pastore has argued in a lecture that "as both metaphors and material substances, slimes [have] appeared along the edges of geographical knowledge, among the frontiers of technology, and near the limits of accepted norms about who should conduct science and where and how it should be conducted" (Pastore 2019). Yet, slime predominantly registers (when it registers at all) in the elemental imaginary as a thing of danger, horror, and disgust. More often, however, slime has simply fallen outside of the range of intellectual control and understanding.

Slime, I will show, is an element that defies the kinds of intellectual and material control that so much of the extractive ethics of science and capitalism embodies. For millennia in the popular imagination, slime has been an elemental intruder, an agent with bad intentions and profound biological and philosophical implications. It slides freely across the borders of the living and the dead, the solid and the liquid, the dangerous and the necessary, evoking responses as varied as terror and horror for some and joy and excitement for others. As entangled with ecophobic fears of nonhuman biological agency as it is with nonbiotic agencies, slime is the unrecognized elemental intruder, the border-crosser *par excellence* whose space is as ambivalent as can be. Its agency is a threat to our own. "We talk about nonhuman agency all the time in everyday life," Susan Heckman explains, summarizing from Andrew Pickering's *Constructing Quarks* (Heckman 2010, 24), but this is often with a defensive reflex whose object is to protect our own agency. Indeed, it is the degree to which biological and nonbiological elements of the natural world (and their

---

[2] It is difficult to imagine *how* they do this. Sheldrake explains of amoeba *Physarum polycephalum* as follows:

> *Physarum* form exploratory networks made of tentacle-like veins and have no central nervous system – nor anything that resembles one. Yet they can "make decisions" by comparing a range of possible courses of action and can find the shortest path between two points in a labyrinth. (Sheldrake 2020, 15)

Exactly how they can do this is simply not known at present.

responses to our assaults) threaten or are perceived to threaten our agency and our lives that forms the substratum of many of these discussions about agency. It is its imagined uncontrollable agency that has made slime so integral to representations of horror, disease, disgust, and abjection. The topic deserves sustained critical attention. Relatively speaking, slime has been absent from Anthropocene and climate change discussions. Anthony Camara noted in 2014 that the "topic has received virtually no attention from scholars outside of specialists in the field of mycology" (Camara 2014, 9). The observation still largely holds. Jean-Paul Sartre offers one of the relatively few serious theoretical investigations of slime, and his meditations get to the heart of slime's ambivalence.[3] Sartre maintains that slime is matter "whose materiality must on principle remain non-meaningful" (Sartre 1966, 605). It is this principle that makes slime an utterly ambivalent site, and this ambivalence makes slime both the matter of fascination to children and matter to which they "show repulsion" (605). Sartre's theoretical discussions of slime are unique, compelling, and informative: "Sliminess proper, considered in its isolated state," he argues, "will appear to us harmful in practice" (605). Slime is a threat. It threatens boundaries, and "the slimy appears as already the outline of a fusion of the world with myself" (606). Slime is a dangerous transcorporeal matter that threatens the very boundaries that it traverses. University of Colorado professor Kelly Hurley has explained that

> Nothing illustrates the Thing-ness of matter so admirably as slime. Nor can anything illustrate the Thing-ness of the human body so well as its sliminess, or propensity to become slime. Slimy substances – excreta, sexual fluids, saliva, mucus – seep from the borders of the body, calling attention to the body's gross materiality. [T. H.] Huxley's description of protoplasm indicates that sliminess is the very essence of the body, and is not just exiled to its borders. Within an evolutionist narrative, human existence has its remote origins in the "primordial slime" from which all life was said to arise. (Hurley 1996, 34)

Seeping from but not exiled to the borders, at the core and origin of the body and yet a matter of profound disgust and horror,[4] slime is beyond our command, is not the water we so proudly control in our fountains and dams: indeed, as Sartre explains, slime "presents itself as a phenomenon in the process of becoming; it does not have the permanence within change that water has but on the contrary represents an accomplished break in a change of state. This fixed instability in

---

[3] "Slime is the agony of water," Jean-Paul Sartre explains (Sartre 1966, 607). One of the few philosophers to try to understand the place of slime in the cultural imagination, Sartre's work has informed much of the work that has followed on the topic.

[4] Noël Carroll argues that there is a "tendency in horror novels and stories to describe monsters in terms of and to associate them with filth, decay, deterioration, slime and so on. The monster in horror fiction, that is, is not only lethal but – and this is of utmost significance – also disgusting" (Carroll 1990, 22).

the slimy discourages possession" (Sartre 1966, 607). It can neither be possessed nor controlled.

After Sartre, the next significant investigation to appear on the topic of slime was Susanne Wedlich's expansive 2019 analysis in *Das Buch vom Schleim*. The 2021 English translation (*Slime: A Natural History*) goes where no book had gone before, either in terms of breadth or in depth of discussions. Wedlich looks at phenomenology, physics, microbial studies, evolution, horror, water, and environment. Written as, to use the author's own words, "a popular science book on slime,"[5] Wedlich's book is accessible and, in important ways, brings slime into discussions long overdue about our current environmental issues. For the most part, slime has not been among the charismatic phyla garnering the attention of environmental activists or well-intentioned ecocritics. The propensity to imagine a vengeful and hostile nature indeed reaches a weird crescendo with slime. Other-than-human agency often evokes responses of ecophobia,[6] and slime is agential elementality at its queerest and most dangerous.

We picture slime as the consummate agent of infection and rot, but it is, in fact, utterly indifferent – and indifference is hard to accept. Priscilla Wald argues that "nothing better illustrates the reluctance to accept Nature's indifference toward human beings and the turn from the ecological analysis in accounts of emerging infections of all varieties than the seemingly irresistible tendency to animate a microbial foe" (Wald 2008, 42). History shows that we find it more palatable to accept hostility than indifference. Perhaps we need the concept of a hostile Nature in order to live well, and perhaps John Durham Peters is right to suggest that "hostile environments breed art" (Peters 2015, 11),[7] but so do sublime and

---

[5] Personal correspondence, May 16, 2022.

[6] I have defined ecophobia elsewhere as follows:

> The ecophobic condition exists on a spectrum and can embody fear, contempt, indifference, or lack of mindfulness (or some combination of these) towards the natural environment. While its genetic origins have functioned, in part, to preserve our species, the ecophobic condition has also greatly serviced growth economies and ideological interests. Often a product of behaviors serviceable in the past but destructive in the present, it is also sometimes a product of the perceived requirements of our seemingly exponential growth. Ecophobia exists globally on both macro and micro levels, and its manifestation is at times directly apparent and obvious but is also often deeply obscured by the clutter of habit and ignorance. (Estok 2018, 2)

I have been careful not to imply that all fear of nature is necessarily ecophobic – a point that Rayson K. Alex and S. Susan Deborah usefully take up, noting in a discussion about eco-fear and eco-reverence in Indigenous communities that "it is not always useful to understand the fearful relation between humans and their ecology as ecophobic" (Alex and Deborah 2019, 423).

[7] Jeffrey Jerome Cohen and Lowell Duckert observe that part of our existence is defined by how we grapple with an environment that we imagine as hostile: "the elements are hostile: nature [is an] adversary, a force to subdue and survive, not to live with" (Cohen and Duckert 2015, 11).

transcendental beauty, grand canyons, and epic waterfalls. It is, of course, the other-than-human *agencies* of environments that make them hostile.

Wedlich's volume is a welcome entry in a field that has hosted some disappointing discussions. Ben Woodard's short 2012 monograph entitled *Slime Dynamics*, for instance, while a promising title on an extremely important topic, seems not to have been either copy-edited or even proof-read. The book has some interesting and quotable moments, to be sure, as Woodard argues "that slime is a viable physical and metaphysical object necessary to produce a realist bio-philosophy void of anthrocentricity [*sic*]" (Woodard 2012, backflap). Woodard usefully contrasts the generative and the degenerative aspects of slime and attempts to talk about the philosophical implications of our ambivalent relationships with slime. The problem is that the book rambles so much that even the most articulate moments (such as the backflap hook) devolve into gibberish. Iaian Hamilton Grant's seemingly more cogent "Being and Slime: The Mathematics of Protoplasm in Lorenz Oken's 'Physio-Philosophy'" ends with a "return to the problem of the separability of mathematics and nature, [which, Grant argues,] we must now pose [. . .] the other way round: *is a slime-free matheme possible?*" (Grant 318, *emphasis* in original).[8] Far from the accessible prose of Wedlich, Grant's "Being and Slime" is so obtuse that one might think it is a copy-cat Sokal Hoax.[9]

These are, however, no times for kidding around – or for being obtuse and incomprehensible. Global oceans continue to lose diversity and become playhouses of slime to such a degree that University of British Columbia marine biologist Daniel Pauly has gone as far to suggest that our era be termed the "Myxocene," the age of slime (Pauly 2010, 61) instead of the Anthropocene. With COVID-19 and the horrors of what Woodard has called "the nightmarish microbial" that "forces life and death into the same generative slime" (Woodard 2012, 19), these investigations are very timely. It is clearly not only disgust at "the nightmarish microbial" slime that patterns our days, since we went through a whole phase in the early 2020s in which we fetishistically rubbed the slime of hand sanitizers on our palms regularly. Work on the importance of microbial studies within the Environmental Humanities, however, has recently been growing and has in many ways opened spaces for theoretical discussions about slime – and slime is important.

---

[8] The problem here is that Grant's "slime-free matheme" is baffling.

[9] In 1996, New York University physicist Alan Sokal submitted a jargon-riddled, nonsensical paper to *Social Text*, a prominent and well-respected journal, in order to test the journal's vetting process and to see if the journal would "publish an article liberally salted with nonsense if (a) it sounded good and (b) it flattered the editors' ideological preconceptions" (Sokal 1996). Entitled "Transgressing the Boundaries: Towards a Transformative Hermeneutics of Quantum Gravity," the paper was accepted. Three weeks later, Sokal revealed the hoax.

Ed Yong, an award-winning science writer for *The Atlantic*, has argued in response to Anthropocene theorizing that one "could equally argue that we are still living in the Microbiocene" (Yong 2016, 8). More than anything else, slime characterizes the Microbiocene. "It's possible," Wedlich explains, "that life has existed on Earth for nearly four billion years, and for most of history slime reigned supreme, a thick seal on the world" (Wedlich 2021, 141). Yet, slime is a substance that has perplexed and horrified, entertained and pleasured, nauseated and disgusted. A plaything for children (hence, the many slime products available as toys and reading material),[10] an asset in the bedroom, and a necessity for life, slime is also the threat of death and degeneration. This awareness of degeneration plays directly into our ecophobic reflex because it is bathed in notions of a vengeful nature (about which I wrote in *The Ecophobia Hypothesis*), a "vision of a Nature that will finally conquer humanity, reclaim all of the world, and remain long after we are gone" (Estok 2018, 66).[11] And, of course, there is some basis for these fears, since it is an inevitability that we will eventually die and decompose and become

---

[10] In a remarkable and sometimes surprising discussion about slime in her original and, in many ways, pioneering *Shakespeare on the Ecological Surface*, Liz Oakley-Brown remarks on how

> about 18 months into the [COVID-19] pandemic, *The Huffington Post* discussed how watching *Tik Tok* and *YouTube* videos of slime allows spectators to "zone out to the sight of hands poking, squishing and pulling multi-color slime like it's taffy. The different sounds emitted by slimes, such as popping and clicking, can lull viewers into a relaxed state." (Flores, as cited by Oakley-Brown 2024, 123. See also Flores 2021)

One of the unexpected things Oakley-Brown points out – something that most of us (myself included) perhaps have not considered – is that recreational slime is environmentally bad: "climate activists rightly question," Oakley-Brown notes, "the production of commercial slime, essentially a plastic substance made for frivolous consumption" (Oakley-Brown 2024, 122. See also "Slime: Can it be environmentally friendly?" 2018).

[11] The theme has become more and more frequent in the late twentieth and early twenty-first centuries. It all may seem innocent enough, a mere comment on Nature's resilience – perhaps even a celebration of it. Roberto Marchesini explains that "the theme of nature taking up the spaces abandoned by the human being, in line with the descriptions of the ecological transformations that took place in Chernobyl, returns in many videos shared on social media showing deer, badgers, wolves, and bears walking peacefully through the city streets" (Marchesini 2021, 15). Yet, these images – like those in the 2007 film *I Am Legend*, as in the Animal Planet/Discovery Channel's joint production of the CGI series *The Future is Wild* (2003), Alan Weisman's 2007 book *The World Without Us*, the History Channel's *Life After People* (January 2008), and the National Geographic Channel's *Aftermath: Population Zero* (March 2008) – remind us of our unimportance. The opening epigraph of the Weisman book is itself horrifying:

> Das Firmament blaut ewig, und die Erde
> Wird lange fest steh'n und aufblüh'n im Lenz.
> Du aber, Mensch, wie lange lebst denn du?

> (The firmament is blue forever, and the Earth
> Will long stand firm and bloom in spring.
> But, man, how long will you live?)
> (Li-Tai-Po/Hans Bethge/Gustav Mahler, *The Chinese Flute: Drinking Song of the Sorrow of the Earth*, Das Lied von der Erde, cited by Weisman 2007, preliminary matter)

slime. This enfolding of life and death in slime threatens the sense of human exceptionalism by asserting that humanity's residence is firmly within and indistinguishable from the material world.

Myxophobia (fear of slime) is perhaps a part of the ecophobic vision of the return of (and perhaps a desperate response to being overwhelmed by) Nature. Philosopher Eugene Thacker understands well the sense of how overwhelming and incomprehensible anthropogenic changes are and argues that the horror of philosophy (not to be confused with the philosophy of horror) is the fact that "the world is increasingly unthinkable" (Thacker 2011, 1). Thacker eloquently comments at the beginning of *In the Dust of this Planet* that

> in spite of our daily concerns, wants, and desires, it is increasingly difficult to comprehend the world in which we live and of which we are a part. To confront this idea is to confront an absolute limit to our ability to adequately understand the world at all – an idea that has been a central motif of the horror genre for some time. (1)

Thacker is careful to explain that his intent is not to define horror but rather to delineate the horror of philosophy,

> the isolation of those moments in which philosophy reveals its own limitations and constraints, moments in which thinking enigmatically confronts the horizon of its own possibility – the thought of the unthinkable that philosophy cannot pronounce but via a nonphilosophical language. (2)

He argues that

> what the genre horror does do is it takes aim at the presuppositions of philosophical inquiry – that the world is always the world-for-us – and makes of those blind spots its central concern, expressing them not in abstract concepts but in a bestiary of impossible life forms – mists, ooze, blobs, slime, clouds, and muck. (9)

There it is: slime. Thacker later describes slime as "being not quite pure nature and yet not quite pure supernature" (55). It is central to horror, along with ooze. In terms useful for theorizing about the elementality of slime, Thacker explains that

> what oozes can be slime, mud, oil, or pus. Ooze can ooze on the body, in the ground, in the sea or in space. Slime, for instance, can be understood in a scientific scene (for instance in plant microbiology or prokaryotic biology), but slime is also something between a liquid and a solid. (83)

Yet, slime is elemental in a way that ooze is not; it is a substrate rather than a predicative thing. Slime is a basis for other things; ooze, on the other hand, can never shake its verbal core and how it predicates an action – namely, a slow, gooey flow – about its subject. Ooze is not the substrate on which things are built; slime is. As Stacy Alaimo has explained, "elements are not things, not objects or artifacts, but that which is the substrate for things, as well as life, to emerge" (Alaimo 2015, 298).[12] This premise is relevant to Cohen and Duckert's idea that the "elemental" is "generative matter" (Cohen and Duckert 2015, 2). The primordial soup that began all life is slime's generative capacity and ontic elementality writ large.

Slime is very different from the other oozes that Thacker mentions, and there does not seem to be a defensible reason for equating ooze and slime in the way that Thacker does. Doing so suggests an elemental quality that ooze simply lacks. Thacker's argument begins to unravel when he explains that "ooze may also be metamorphic and shapeshifting, as with the organisms classed as *myxomycota*" (Thacker 2011, 83). While the Greek origin of the word *myxo-mycota* (*myxo*) means *mucus* or *slime*, and while mucus can be either slime or ooze, slime itself has come to mean something different than ooze. It cannot be a verb like ooze: to be clear, then, the two are *not* synonyms.[13] It is more than simply a semantic disagreement here. Thacker explains that "horror is also replete with ooze. Ooze always seems to attach itself to monsters, dripping off their tendrils and making them all the more abject and repulsive" (88). This description, however, is simply inaccurate. It is not ooze that drips from mother Alien's mouth: it is slime. Ooze lacks the elemental tactility and affect of slime. Lava can be ooze, but it cannot be slime. Slime is the basis of many different things, including life and rot; not so with ooze. It is not ooze that covers the creature from the black lagoon: it is slime. This semantic issue notwithstanding, Thacker's claim that ooze is often an agent of a vengeful nature is an important one (90). Again, however, it is the elementality of slime that makes its agential nature the more frightening. As one of the preconditions of life, slime ought not to turn against such life, and thinking that slime could indeed do so generates horror. It is an ecophobic notion of unnaturalness (perhaps akin to the idea of a cannibalistic parent),[14] and imagining a vengeful slime ratchets up the horror. The idea of an agential and vengeful nature comes up again and again with slime and its vectors, but the reality is that while it is agential, it is not vengeful – and ideas that it is are simply anthropocentric anxieties venting themselves in

---

[12] To suggest, however, that being a substrate obviates "thingness" is at variance with the major elemental theories of Empedocles, Plato, and Aristotle.

[13] Even so, their etymological origins suggest a synonymity that has since slid into difference. According to W.W. Skeat, both words – though from different origins – signified "mud" ("ooze" from the Anglo-Saxon and Icelandic words "wōs" and "vās," respectively, and "slime" from the Latin word "līmus").

[14] See also Section 3.1, in which I briefly discuss that cannibalistic actions of a character (a woman eating her "offspring") in a Hiromi Goto short story.

anthropomorphic metaphors. But reality and how we envision it are two very different things.

Sartre's understanding is that "immediately the slimy reveals itself as essentially ambiguous," and "nothing testifies more clearly to its ambiguous character as a 'substance between two states' than the slowness with which the slimy melts into itself" (Sartre 1966, 606, 607). Dan Brayton explains that in Shakespeare's day, "slime, like magic, was a phenomenon imbued with all sorts of impending explanations – indeed, it would be reasonable to describe slime as the objective correlative of early modern epistemological uncertainty" (Brayton 2015, 88). For Brayton, "Shakespearean representations of slime and its cousin ooze can be seen to represent an index and obscure prologue to modern ecological thought, in general, and ecocriticism in particular" (81). Brayton's comments about early modern representations of slime are important and reflect an understanding that "slime has occupied the conceptual space between matter and life, that unfathomable substance figured variously as chaos, *noumenon*, and primal soup which precedes and interrogates our notions of that which is empirically real – and alive" (81). For Brayton, these thoughts hold as true in the early modern period as they do in the Anthropocene, and slime remains essential in how we apprehend the material world. Far from being an element of concern to people of the distant past, to Shakespeare and his contemporary physicians and epidemiologists, slime is a matter of dangers and ambivalences, with relevance to contemporary conversations about misogyny, racism, and class. Slime connects and disconnects us, to each other and to the world. Slime is political. Its ubiquity is palpable, and its dearth in discussions within the environmental humanities, pronounced. Understanding how we recognize and mediate this element can help us to move forward.

Slime: An Elemental Imaginary takes up challenges laid down by several authors. One of these challenges is from Brayton to trace "a literary-intellectual genealogy of slime," a substance that "in Shakespeare," Brayton notes, "emblematizes human efforts to understand and manipulate the biophysical environment" (81). Another challenge is to address what Susanne Wedlich calls "slime blindness" (Wedlich 2021, 3) and to understand the history of slime. This is a massive and genuinely interdisciplinary undertaking, spanning the natural and social sciences, and riveted in narratives both scientific and fictional. The goal here is to understand slime within what Melody Jue and Rafico Ruiz call "an elemental scholarship that exceeds the solidity of earth, the fluidity of water, the temperature sensitivity of fire, and the mobility of air" (Jue and Ruiz 2021, 5).

In this Element, I will approach slime through four topics: its agencies, its connections and entanglements (which are obviously separate but overlapping topics), and its diversions (both originary and causal), with a brief discussion of the increasing relevance of slime in the rich and developing discipline that has come to be known as "the Blue Humanities." In the "Postscript," I will slide along the carcass of one whale and through the semen of another to offer a few final words on slime's pervasive presence in eco-horror, the ecogothic, disgust, and disruptive emergences.

1 Agencies

1.1 New Materialism and Emergence

> To limit the discussion to humans, their interests, their subjectivities, and their rights, will appear as strange a few years from now as having denied the right to vote of slaves, poor people, or women. (Bruno Latour 2004, 69)

One of the greatest insights of the New Material turn has been to popularize the notion of nonhuman agency. For New Materialists, agency is an inherent aspect of materials themselves and is not the sole domain of the human, and there is a lot at stake in such a radical proposition. Indeed, as Diana Coole and Samantha Frost explain in their introduction to *New Materialisms: Ontology, Agency, and Politics*, "what is at stake here is nothing less than a challenge to some of the most basic assumptions that have underpinned the modern world, including its normative sense of the human and its beliefs about human agency, but also regarding its material practices such as the ways we labor on, exploit, and interact with nature" (Coole and Frost 2010, 4).

In their monumental collection entitled *Material Ecocriticism* that features applications of the New Materialism to ecocritical approaches and the Environmental Humanities, Serenella Iovino and Serpil Oppermann explain that

> Agency assumes many forms, all of which are characterized by an important feature: they are *material*, and the meanings they produce influence in various ways the existence both of human and nonhuman natures. Agency, therefore, is not to be necessarily and exclusively associated with human beings and with human intentionality, but is a pervasive and inbuilt property of matter, as part and parcel of its generative dynamism. From this dynamism, reality emerges as an intertwined flux of material and discursive forces, rather than as [a] complex of hierarchically organized individual players. (Iovino and Oppermann 2014, 3)

Now more than ever, these issues of "material ecocriticism" are imperative for understanding our climate crises, and much of the work in this emerging area is necessarily inter- and transdisciplinary. At the start of the third decade of the twenty-first century, we were reminded perhaps like never before of just how much a mistake it is to ignore the impacts of materiality and nonhuman material agencies on our daily lives. Climate change realities, which had begun to receive long-overdue mass media attention until 2020, suddenly became low on the list of priorities in the public imagination, with the staggering material realities of the COVID-19 pandemic trumping virtually everything else in our day-to-day lives. The agency of a microscopic material would bring the airline industry to its knees, cost the world trillions of dollars in losses, infect and kill millions of people, and produce untold numbers of unknown effects.[15] Elemental agencies are clearly in need of a lot of attention.

Summarizing from the growing body of work in new material studies, Moritz Ingwersen and Timo Müller explain that "the material world is anything but inert" and that there are "two intersecting lines of argumentation":

> One is to decenter the human and recognize nonhumans as agential actors in their own right with an inherent material vibrancy and capacity to affect and shape their surroundings. Understood in this way as the generative and po(i)etic potential intrinsic to all matter, agency becomes a property of matter that fundamentally challenges conceptions of 'nature' or 'things' as inert substances or passive tools dependent on human activation. The other line of argumentation is to reconceive agency not as a property inherent to individualized entities – human or nonhuman – but as an emergent, collective, and relational feature of networks or assemblages of material-semiotic practices and forces. (Ingwersen and Müller 2022, 12)

In *Emergence: the Connected Lives of Ants, Brains, Cities, and Software*, Steven Johnson defines "emergence" as "the movement from low-level rules to higher-level sophistication" (Johnson 2004,18). Slimes offer a way into these discussions. Johnson explains that

> the slime mold spends much of its life as thousands of distinct single-celled units, each moving separately from its comrades. Under the right conditions, those myriad cells will coalesce again into a single, larger organism, which then begins its leisurely crawl across the garden floor, consuming rotting leaves and wood as it moves about. (13)

It is transmorphic: "The slime mold oscillates between being a single creature and a swarm" (13). The morphing of slime from single creatures to a kind of collective intelligence bears a startling resemblance to what Melody Jue describes as at least one of the visions of blue feminist materialisms: "The posthuman subject that emerges from these watery feminist materialisms should change our self-conception, encouraging us to see our own distributed embodiment as a condition that is attached to the ecological welfare of a sphere larger than our own body" (Jue 2020, 20).

---

[15] This sentence and the preceding two appear in slightly different forms in Estok 2020, 591–92.

One reason slime so consistently evokes a sense of horror may have something to do with how it conflicts with our sense of causes and effects, how it refutes the notion of leadership and hierarchy, and how it defies expectations about collective organization:[16] "Much of the world around us," Johnson notes, "can be explained in terms of command systems and hierarchies – why should it be any different for the slime molds?" (Johnson 2004, 15). Yet, it is different, and what he describes as "the eerie, invisible hand of self-organization" (16)[17] is more than simply eerie; it is a threat to our sense of order. Johnson explains how Evelyn Fox Keller came to resist "the conventional belief [. . .] that slime mold swarms formed at the command of 'pace-maker' cells that ordered the other cells to begin aggregating" (14). Keller, Johnson notes, built on the work of one of Alan Turing's last published papers about "how a complex organism could assemble itself without any master planner calling the shots" (14). Grasping such an idea has never been easy.

1.2 Grasping for Slime

Perhaps it is slime's elemental amorphousness and definitional intractability that make it an attractive ingredient in imagining horror. The very notion of slimic agency indeed is the stuff of horror films, with slime dripping from the mouths of aliens or covering or devouring or transforming people's bodies in films such as *The Blob* (1958), *The Thing* (1982), *The Fly* (1986 remake), *Alien* (virtually the entire franchise), *Poltergeist* (1982), *Demons* (1985), *Street Trash* (1987), *Troll 2* (1990), *Frankenstein* (1994), and so on. Because slime is also deeply entangled with gender, race, and class in the popular imagination, as I will show, it is important to analyze these issues in tandem with matters of slimic agency and slime's elemental amorphousness.

There has been a surge of interest within the past decade or so in elemental theory,[18] yet slime seems to ooze out of reach in many discussions. This is odd, because slime is never far away from us – from our origins in primordial slime to the slime of copulation that initiates our conception, it is elemental in our existence. While it clearly does not fall firmly within any of the four

---

[16] I address this further below (in Section 3.2) with a few brief comments about the relationship between matters of uniformity and loss of diversity, on the one hand, with individuality on the other.

[17] This sounds very similar to Albert Einstein's famous comment about quantum entanglements and the capacity (indeed inevitability) of matter to interact at a distance with other matter. Einstein called it "Spukhafte Fernwirkungen" ("spooky actions at a distance"). See Born 1971, 159.

[18] Cohen and Duckert, in their introduction to the collection *Elemental Ecocriticism: Thinking with Earth, Air, Water, and Fire*, make a succinct and clear point that theorizing about elementality is "not arguing for the uncritical embrace of outmoded epistemologies [. . .] not a project of nostalgia, not a wistful retreat from present-day concerns into supposedly simpler cosmogenies" (Cohen and Duckert 2015, 4) but is a re-visiting of what has been perhaps too readily abandoned. They ask, "how did we forget that matter is a precarious system and dynamic entity, not a reservoir of tractable commodities?" (5).

Empedoclean elements (water, air, earth, and fire), slime is, nevertheless, a component of life – and of eco-horror. Slime is an element whose dimensions have occupied philosophers for millennia, and there is, now more than ever before, an urgency to address the profound environmental, political, and social dimensions of slimic agency.

There is a long literary history representing the dangers of agential slime. Early modern medicinal writings uniformly associate slime with disease and disorders. Thomas O'Dowde's 1664 *A Poor Man's Medicine* associates infections of the blood with slime; Thomas (AKA Tobias) Venner's 1638 *Via Recta* links poorly prepared foods (fish in particular) with the production of unwholesome slime and disease; and countless other contemporaries of Shakespeare, building on the humoral theories of Galen, announce the dangerous and unhealthful properties of slime. So prevalent are these documents that Shakespeare himself has much to say on the topic of slime. *Othello* has Iago announce that "An honest man he is, and hates the slime / That sticks on filthy deeds" (5.2.155–156). In *Richard III*, slime is clearly associated with death when Clarence dreams about drowning and going down to "the slimy bottom of the deep" (1.4.32). As in our own time, however, slime in the early modern period is at best ambivalent, both symbolic of death and life, rot and fertility, good and bad.

In *Great Expectations*, the "old hulls of ships in course of being knocked to pieces" float amid the "ooze and slime and other dregs of tide" (Dickens 1980, 369). Here slime is part of the dissolution of the human into the natural worlds and of the reclamation of the materials wrought by the human hand. In Charlotte Brontë's *Jane Eyre*, slimic agency takes on a nationalist flavor. Slime here is associated with English nationalism, "the slime and mud of Paris" an implicit threat that contrasts with the "clean [. . .], wholesome soil of an English country garden" (Brontë 1971, 127). Slime is more explicitly agential in its relation with contagion and disease in *Bleak House*. It manifests as the "odious slime" of a frog in *Gulliver's Travels* and is, at another point in the narrative, part of the origin of two "brutes" who "appeared together upon a mountain; whether produced by the heat of the sun upon corrupted mud and slime, or from the ooze and froth of the sea, was never known" (Swift 1960, 97; 219). Moreover, as it is physically ambivalent, so too is it conceptually slippery. While it pollutes, infects, and endangers, at other times it cures.

The ambivalences of slime become more pronounced than ever as science advances and new models of understanding develop. One of the interesting hypotheses (subsequently borne out by scientific research) was about the meliorative and medicinal properties of snail and mollusk slime. While such ideas go all the way back to the Greeks and Romans, one source explains that in the 18th century [slime] was recommended as a treatment for anthrax, and in the 19th century for tuberculosis. 'Snail broth' made from the mucus was said to encourage the regeneration of wounded skin, reduce redness and make skin smoother. (Pitt 2019, 1)

There are more ominous imagined effects of agential slime, however, and these find a truly spectacular expression in Samuel Taylor Coleridge's *The Rime of the Ancient Mariner*. Yet, it is more the slime of justice than of malice that we witness here. After all, nature becomes hostile *in response* to the Mariner's crime, and this response of antagonism and vengeance is in large part mediated through slime. Much of this vengeance involves leaving the mariner rudderless, unable to control his movement through the elements – in part because those very elements have lost their referential stability. It is hard to nail down slime.[19]

With the rise of the gothic novel, the connections between slime and horror become fixed. In Robert Louis Stevenson's *Dr. Jekyll and Mr. Hyde*, human agency dissolves into slime, and Dr. Jekyll "thought of Hyde, for all his energy of life, as of something not only hellish but inorganic. This was the shocking thing; that the slime of the pit seemed to utter cries and voices" (Stevenson 2003, 60). Part of the horror here is the agency of slime, its capacity to make sounds. The agency of nonhuman materials is often the source of horror, of course. It is agency that makes monsters monstrous.

One of the greatest horror classics of all time – Mary Shelley's *Frankenstein* – surprisingly has no slime at all; even so, there is something about the story that inspires the slimic imagination, as is very clear in the 1994 Kenneth Branagh filmic version with Robert DeNiro. The "wretch" is borne of a tub of slime, re-membered from the dead, a man not of woman born, yet carried to term (as it were) in a kind of a womb (a huge tub), all the while floating in a ghastly slime (rather than in amniotic fluid) that explodes into a chaotic and very slippery mess at the moment of his "birth." At least part of the horror in these narratives is in the unnaturalness and subsequent danger that slime represents. It is imagined to go against nature and is "associated with the threat and uncertainty of boundaries and borders, [...] the boundary between life and death" (Brayton 2015, 87). Resolutely an environmental issue, slime in many ways *is* horror.

In Arthur Machen's "The Great God Pan," the horrific agency of slime touches several registers. For one thing, it stands centrally as a symbol of a clearly dangerous and demonized female sexuality. All of the slimic disgust and horror in the novella centers on Helen, the main character, and she eventually goes through a kind of backward evolution – what Machen calls "Protoplasmic reversion" (Machen 2018, 144) – and dissolves into a puddle

---

[19] I deal more expansively with *The Rime of the Ancient Mariner* in Section 1.4.

of slime. Machen plays on both the fear of slime and on the sexist contempt for women's agency in his audience here. Another register Machen touches is our own ontological insecurities and fears that our place in the scheme of things is far from guaranteed.

Backward evolution is a recurring theme in Machen and always involves slime. It happens also to Francis Leicester in a subsection of Machen's "The Three Imposters" entitled "Novel of the White Powder." Leicester becomes slime, "a dark and putrid mass seething with corruption and rottenness, neither liquid nor solid, but melting and changing before our eyes and bubbling with unctuous oily bubbles" (Machen 2018, 172). In another subsection (entitled "Novel of the Black Seal") of "The Three Imposters," a boy (who, incidentally, is the offspring of a woman and the god Pan) falls sick and, while "foaming at the mouth" on the floor, "horror broke" as "something pushed out from the body there on the floor, and stretched forth a slimy wavering tentacle, across the room" (142). He seems to be another case of "protoplasmic reversion." One thing is certain: slime and horror go together here.

As a genre, horror involves the agency of nature just beyond control and domestication. It is the unexpected and the uncontrolled. Horror is the boundary-crosser. It is the defiance of the elements, of order, and of safety. It is the uncanny convergence of meaning across changing elemental media, "the agony of water" as it moves slimeward. To know the powers of horror is to know the appeal of the repulsive and to understand the draw of those things Julia Kristeva describes that do "not respect borders, positions, rules. The in-between, the ambiguous, the composite" (Kristeva 1982, 4). It is an appeal and repulsion not simply of elemental crossings and contradictions but of the very fact of such agonistic relationships, such possibilities of both degeneration and regeneration embodied in one substance – and the danger in it all both thrills and horrifies.

1.3 Slimic Agency: Ecogothic and Horror

Ecology without nature is dandy, but ecocriticism without science is dangerous. (Lee Rozelle 2016, 8)

. . . slime molds have no monopoly on brainless problem solving, but they are easy to study and have become poster organisms that have opened up new avenues of research. (Sheldrake 2020,15)

Humankind is deeply ill. The species won't last long. It was an aberrant experiment. Soon the world will be returned to the healthy intelligences, the collective ones. Colonies and hives. (Powers 2018, 70)

Powers mentions colonies and hives, and we need to add slime molds. Slime is part of the stock-and-trade of horror and the ecogothic, and there are solid bases on which to ground our worries about intelligent and potentially threatening slime.[20] Unless we are to play fast and free with the notion of intelligence, however, it is useful to examine some definitions of the term. According to University of Michigan computer scientist Peter Lindes, "Intelligence is the ability of an agent, whether human, animal, artificial, or something else, to act in its environment in real time, using its limited knowledge, memory, computational power, and perception and action capabilities, choosing actions at each moment that move it toward its current goals, and to adapt over time by improving this ability to act" (Lindes 2020, 2). This definition stands in contrast to "the prevailing scientific view," which, Merlin Sheldrake explains, "is that it is a mistake to imagine that there is anything deliberate about most nonhuman interactions" (Sheldrake 2020, 41). Such a view leaves no viable categorical space for the actions of slime molds. As Steven Johnson observes, "For scientists trying to understand systems that use relatively simple components to build higher-level intelligence, the slime mold may someday be seen as the equivalent of the finches and tortoises that Darwin observed on the Galápagos Islands" (Johnson 2004, 11–12). For anyone who has ever been lost in an IKEA store and stuck following the arrows of what seems like a giant IKEA assembly instruction booklet, what Sheldrake explains about the intelligence of slime can only be humbling:

> Japanese researchers released slime molds into petri dishes modeled on the Greater Tokyo area. Oat flakes marked major urban hubs and bright lights represented obstacles such as mountains – slime molds don't like light. After a day, the slime mold had found the most efficient route between the oats, emanating into a network almost identical to Tokyo's existing rail network. In similar experiments, slime molds have re-created the motorway network of the United States and the network of Roman roads in central Europe. A slime-mold enthusiast told me about a test he had performed. He frequently got lost in IKEA stores and would spend many minutes trying to find the exit. He decided to challenge his slime molds with the same problem and built a maze based on the floor plan of his local IKEA. Sure enough, without any signs or staff to direct them, the slime molds soon found the shortest path to the exit. (Sheldrake 2020, 15)

---

[20] Threats from slime are an increasingly present topic of scholarly discussion. Several articles in the 2023 *Studies in American Fiction* Special Double Issue on the "Ecogothic" touch on the issue. Echoing Sartre's idea that slime is "the agony of water," Joshua Myers explains that "mold and the conditions that grow it are ghostly reminders of water's past" (Myers 2023, 12) and that "a fungal presence speaks to the ecogothic because it embodies the most ancient of human fears: that of being preyed upon" (16). For Patrick Whitmarsh, the potential danger is in "the slimy uncertainty of the swamp" (Whitmarsh 2023, 161), and for Matthew Wynn Sivils, it is in "feculent pools" (Sivils 2023, 1). Indeed, ecogothic anxieties are often, as this volume shows, immersed in slime.

Sheldrake's questions on the topic seem to me very important: "Are network-based life-forms like fungi or slime molds capable of a form of cognition? Can we think of their behavior as intelligent? If other organisms' intelligence didn't look like ours, then how might it appear? Would we even notice it?" (65). While the answers to these questions are indeed extensive and complicated, it seems – at least following the definition Lindes offers – that the ability to make choices, to act as an agent (to have agency), must be central to our understanding of what it means to *have* intelligence.

The slime in Jeff VanderMeer's *Annihilation* is horrifying because it seems smart:

> ... if it has intelligence, that intelligence is far different from our own. It creates out of our ecosystem a new world, whose processes and aims are utterly alien – one that works through supreme acts of mirroring, and by remaining hidden in so many other ways, all without surrendering the foundations of its *otherness* as it becomes what it encounters. (VanderMeer 2014, 191)

Tara Wanda Merrigan describes *Annihilation* as a "book about an intelligent, deadly fungus" (Merrigan 2014). It is the intelligence and the willfulness of slime that seem beyond our control and therefore produce horror.[21]

Even when not directly described, slime invokes horror. In Yann Martel's *The Life of Pi*, for instance, there is much that could evoke horror – not the least of which is having to share a lifeboat with a hungry, full-grown 450-pound Bengal tiger. Yet, this charismatic carnivore with its big sharp teeth is a kind of slapstick horror compared to the toothless slime that almost appears on the island where Pi and Richard Parker (the tiger) land. There is something eerie about "the island's complete desolation," save for the "shining green algae" (Martel 2001, 300; 301), the meerkats, and the dead fish in the pulsating pond. Eerie, however, is not horror. The horror comes wrapped in oyster slime:

---

[21] In many ways, the slimic and fungal imaginations are deeply entangled with each other, in part because slime is so much more obviously central to the realities of fungal existence than it is to, say, our own. As Sheldrake explains, "Although they're not fungi, slime molds have evolved ways to coordinate their sprawling, shape-shifting bodies and provide a helpful model for thinking about the challenges and opportunities faced by mycelial fungi" (Sheldrake 2020, 246). Among these challenges and opportunities are the possibilities of both degeneration and regeneration. These dual possibilities evoke responses that Christy Tidwell has identified as a "tension between fear and hope" (Tidwell 2023, 246). Tidwell's understanding of fungi is nuanced: "They frighten us, but they also offer an opportunity for change" (247), she explains. Citing from Anna Lowenhaupt Tsing, Tidwell explains that fungi "change who we are" and make us "remember that changing with circumstances is the stuff of survival" (Tsing 2015, 27 as cited by Tidwell 2023, 247). And slime is inextricable from the character make-up of fungi. For Ashley Kniss, fungi "are a source of horror and repulsion, an alien life form, proliferating as a slime-mold and grotesque fruiting bodies, some masquerading as edible prizes with deadly results" (Kniss 2023, 249).

at the heart of a green oyster. A human tooth. A molar, to be exact. The surface stained green and finely pierced with holes. The feeling of horror came slowly. [Pi] had time to pick at the other fruit. Each contained a tooth. One a canine. Another a premolar. Here an incisor. There another molar. Thirty-two teeth. A complete human set. Not one tooth missing. Understanding dawned upon [him. He] did not scream. [He thought] only in movies is horror vocal. [He] simply shuddered and left the tree. (Martel 2001, 311)

The slime here is not so toothless after all. The horror here, however, is wrapped in slime that does not actually appear, since the "green oyster" is a metaphor and not truly an oyster. Even so, the first thing most people think of with oysters is either something sexual (that they are an aphrodisiac)[22] or something about slime – or both. The mention of oysters and all that they evoke, along with teeth, brings to mind – whether or not Martel intended it – the vagina dentata image (about which more later in the text). While Pi inadvertently stumbles on a dangerously carnivorous, slimy plant out on the wild and open sea, Coleridge's ancient mariner inadvertently *invites* slimic horrors through his deeds on the wild seas – specifically through his shooting of the albatross.

1.4 The Slime of the Ancient Mariner

A year before the COVID-19 pandemic began, I wrote about *The Rime of the Ancient Mariner* and the importance of slime as an environmental signal in it.[23] Then when the pandemic struck, James Parker of *The Atlantic* wrote a startling article entitled "The 1798 Poem That Was Made for 2020. 'The Rime of the Ancient Mariner' is taking on new meaning during the coronavirus pandemic." In many ways, Parker's title offers a valid statement, and yet the article makes no mention of the slime in the poem, focusing instead on the listlessness we face in confronting unknown terrors and desolation. The failure even to mention slime is all the more extraordinary because of how slime is so central to the horror of the poem; yet, sliminess *per se* is not the actual source of the horror: it is the agency of the slimy things in the poem that evokes fear and revulsion. It is the proximity to the narrating subject of "slimy things [that] did crawl with legs,/ Upon the slimy sea" (Coleridge 1999, ll.12–6) that terrifies. This proximity is clearly not only physical but also ontological: the narrator explains that "a thousand thousand slimy things/ Lived on" (ll.238–9), adding "and so did I" (1.239). The threat here is that the slime and the

---

[22] According to an article posted by Natalie Olsen on *Medical News Today*, "Oysters are among the most famous aphrodisiacs in history. Their effects may be due to their zinc content." It may also have something to do with their morphic and aromal evocation of female genitalia.

[23] Parts of this paragraph appear in different form in that article (Estok 2019).

narrator might be or become indistinguishable.[24] It is a point that William Ian Miller makes in his monumental *Anatomy of Disgust*: "stickiness and sliminess horrify because they erase the distinction between subject and object" (Miller 1997, 271, n.5). So, while, as Miller states, "many different cultures [. . .] converge in agreement that slime and ooze, feces and menstrual blood, are on the polluting side of the equation" (62) and that the polluting aspect of slime is disgusting, it is the agential characteristic that is threatening. Other critics have noted the threat of erasure in the poem, to be sure. Tim Fulford discusses the "zombie" politics of the poem and how "in touching his nephew's living corpse, the mariner violates another taboo – that which separates the living from the dead" (Fulford 2006, 51). Useful as it is, however, Fulford's discussion makes no mention of slime, let alone of its pivotal importance to the poem's questioning of human exceptionalism. This threat of erasure *The Rime of the Ancient Mariner* offers in its depictions of slime, moreover, is *willful*. What the poem imagines is a retributive natural world, a response of nature to the apparently senseless and unwarranted killing of the albatross[25] – and it is precisely this imagining of a hostile, antagonistic, and vengeful nature that situates the poem firmly within a long tradition of ecophobic environmental ethics. We witness a nature beyond our control, and it scares us.

1.5 Resisting Containment

> However critical this dirty work may be to the planet and people, it is our unease with the dark and unknown, with that which dwells underground and consumes the dead, that nevertheless makes us fear the fungal, and which can escalate in media representation into complete ecophobic dread. (Woolbright 2023, 240)

VanderMeer's slime seems to undulate (VanderMeer 2014, 54). Echoes of Charlotte Perkins Gilman's "The Yellow Wallpaper" ricochet through *Annihilation*. Gilman's

---

[24] Indeed, as Karl Kroeber explains, though without reference to the poem's slimic imagery, "human action and human values" are in a struggle for survival in "a natural world animated by supernatural creatures" (Kroeber 1957, 180). Kroeber is a significant voice in early environmental criticism, having proposed "an ecologically oriented literary criticism" (Kroeber 1994, 1) a solid two years before "ecocriticism" officially began with the publication of Lawrence Buell's *The Environmental Imagination* and Cheryll Glotfelty and Harold Fromm's *The Ecocriticism Reader*. The term "ecocriticism" had been around since William Rueckert's 1978 essay entitled "Literature and Ecology: An Experiment in Ecocriticism" but was "apparently [. . .] dormant in [the] critical vocabulary until the 1989 Western Literature Association meeting (in Coeur d'Alene), when Cheryll Glotfelty [. . .] revived the term [. . . and] urged its adoption" (Branch and O'Grady 1994).

[25] For William Empson, the action is neither senseless nor unwarranted: "Nobody who had been reading travellers' reports in bulk could doubt the motive of the Mariner [in shooting the albatross . . .]; he shot it for food" (Empson 1964, 300). Even so, whatever the motive of this fictional character, the poem clearly offers it as a criminal act of unwarranted and unexpected violence, and Empson himself admits that he is "not denying that Coleridge said the Mariner had committed a crime" (301).

narrator sees what others cannot, and the story "pushes its readers to see beyond what is visible, both metaphorically and literally, at one and the same time calling into question what it means to see the unseen and what it means not to see it" (Estok 2023a, 75).[26] Gilman's narrator addresses the reader directly, asking us to "imagine a toadstool in joints, an interminable string of toadstools, budding and sprouting in endless convolutions" (Gilman 1995, 608) and moments later tells us (after pulling off some wallpaper) that "waddling fungus growths just shriek with derision!" (611). This theme about perception runs through *Annihilation*, and VanderMeer's narrator also addresses the reader very directly, at one point apologizing for "not [having] been entirely honest thus far" and hoping that "you might find me a credible, objective witness" (VanderMeer 2014, 55). The narrator expresses regret over having "neglected to mention some details" and worries about "any reader's initial opinion in judging my objectivity" (150) – and, in both Gilman's and VanderMeer's narratives, the reasons the reader might doubt the reliability of the narrators is that they claim to see things others do not. The unnamed narrator of *Annihilation* confesses that there are "things only I could see" (48), shocking things that no rational person would believe. She sees words made of fungi lining the walls of the tunnel they descend. The unnamed anthropologist responds in disbelief: "Words? Words?" (23). So too does the unnamed surveyor: "Words? Made of fungi? [...] This is a joke, right?" (25, 26). Later, the narrator explains to the surveyor that "something I see that you don't might be important" (42). She explains "that the walls were made of living tissue" (42). Both narrators see things that others do not and therefore worry about their reliability as narrators.[27]

One of the issues that VanderMeer tackles is the whole notion of containment – a notion that slime is good at evading, both physically and intellectually. Indeed, part of what VanderMeer is exposing is what David Ehrenfeld has called "the arrogance of humanism" and "our unquestioning humanistic faith in our own omnipotence [, ... our] ability to confront and solve the many problems that humans face, [the] ability to rearrange both the world of Nature and the affairs of men and women so that human life will prosper" (Ehrenfeld 1981, xiii; 5).

---

[26] Gilman was, in a sense, far ahead of her time with questions about "seeing" and "hearing" what nonhuman nature has to communicate. The topic of seeing the unseen and hearing the unheard has become more urgent in popular fiction recently. Listening to the layers of stories in forests and to "how much they say, when you let them" (Powers 2018, 613) is a central theme of the 2018 Richard Powers novel *The Overstory*. Yet, the idea is not so new, and traditional cultures have long held a value for such seeing and listening. An indigenous man from the Pacific Northwest in the novel explains, "We've been trying to tell you that since 1492" (613).

[27] I have stated elsewhere (Estok 2023a, 79) that "seeing something that others cannot see is not *ipso facto* a sign of psychosis; otherwise, stereograms would be a diagnostic tool among psychiatrists." Even so, if someone is stroking an imaginary dog on a subway or chatting animatedly to thin air, there may indeed be something wrong. The narrators in each story have just cause for worrying about their reliability.

When each new expedition goes into "Area X" in *Annihilation*, they do so with all of the surety of the scientist. The fungal slime thing challenges that surety. It communicates in a way that "no recorded human language" does (VanderMeer 2014, 25). The beast that lurks in the marshes, the narrator explains, can be catalogued: "We were confident that eventually we would photograph it, document its behavior, tag it, and assign it a place in the taxonomy of living things. It would become known" (31). The fungal slime thing "would not," however, become known in such a way (31). The irony that VanderMeer reveals is that seeing what others cannot see may ultimately reveal that there is much more that is unseen than seen and that the inadequacy of our perceptions is under-acknowledged. The question is simple: "What can you do when your five senses are not enough" (178). Our senses are unequal to the scale of things.

Scholars have sought to address scalar issues in a variety of ways: Timothy Morton with "hyperobjects;" Rob Nixon with "slow violence;" Dipesh Chakrabarty with "species history;" and Paul Crutzen and Eugene Stoermer with the notion of the "Anthropocene." Richard Powers explains through one of his characters that "we are not [. . .] wired to see slow, background change, when something bright and colorful is waving in our faces" (Powers 2018, 467). Nor are we wired to comprehend slimic agency when all we can see as the vehicle of intelligence and agency are big flashy brains, such as we proudly carry around. Perhaps, then, we are also wired (or, at the very least, inclined) to see and imagine slime – with its cellular uniformity and lack of a brain – as stupid and inactive. This could in part explain why slime's agency is so threatening.

2 Connections

2.1 Shakespeare and the Early Moderns

Slime is a biological substance with physical properties and biological functions. But it is also a phenomenon or an idea which repels and excludes. This has made it an object of disgust in popular culture, be it in literature, in comics or in film. In recent decades, monsters of all kinds can be found leaving extraordinarily slippery trails of slime. Slime has entertainment value, but in playing with our aversions it also offers a kind of lusty frisson. Disgust, one of the most basic of emotions, is intended to protect us from pathogens and infections, but we feel it in response to much more than potential microbial contaminants. Disgust at the crossing of social boundaries can spark discrimination. At worst, people and even whole groups are stigmatized. A long and inglorious tradition has seen women forced into this category – as the apparently slimier sex. (Susanne Wedlich 2021, 9)

Unsurprisingly, fears about slime are entangled with sexism and misogyny – each, to differing degrees, obsessed with power and control. Indeed, myxophobia is deeply enmeshed with the fear of women's bodies and sexuality[28] and with fantasies of violence. Shakespeare offers a great many descriptions of female genitalia, often implicitly and in phobic relation to the environment, or, more specifically, to the land – whence, the "loathsome pit" of *Titus Andronicus* (2.3.193),[29] the "sulphurous pit" of *King Lear* (4.6.125), and the "cold valley-fountain" of *Sonnet 153* (l. 4). The images are far from uniform, ranging from the "no thing" between a fair maid's legs of *Hamlet* (3.2.121) – perhaps out of which derives that "indistinguished space of woman's will" (*King Lear*, 4.6.271) – to the "the dark and vicious place" in which Gloucester begot Edmund in *King Lear* (5.3.173). In the early modern male imagination, the vagina is a place of fluids and slimes that cause corruption, decay, and poisoning. It is a place of dangerous slimic agency.

King Lear clearly exhibits fear and loathing of the vagina when, disgusted with women's agency almost to the point of speechlessness, he rants about what he sees as the source and site of that agency, something that for him and men of his ilk is the most dangerous thing in women:

> Down from the waist they are Centaurs,
> Though women all above.
> But to the girdle do the gods inherit.
> Beneath is all the fiends'; there's hell, there's darkness,
> There's the sulphurous pit, burning, scalding,
> Stench, consumption! Fie, fie, fie! Pah! pah! (4.6.121–26)

The disgust here is palpable. It grows not merely out of a staging of *vagina dentata* misogyny, a fear of loss of masculine control to the sexual volition of women, a fear that dates back to the ancient Greeks; rather, this disgust is a more profound existential worry that the materiality of the vagina engenders in him – a fear of envelopment, death, and dissolution, a fear that grows out of a kind of myxophobia. Lear is getting on in years, is anxious to put things in order and to secure his place, but everything is falling apart, and at the height of it all, he rants about the vagina, the site and source of so much that he fears. His vaginophobia is consonant with early modern men's ideas about menstruation. In her detailed and comprehensive *Menstruation and the Female Body in Early Modern England*, Sara Read offers an expanded discussion of the various links between menstruation and notions of monstrosity in Shakespeare's day.

---

[28] Greta Gaard usefully discusses this fear of sexuality (erotophobia) in relation to sexism, heterosexism, and homophobia (Gaard 1997), as well as in relation to ecophobia: "erotophobia is [. . .] a component of ecophobia" (Gaard 2010, 650); "ecophobia and erotophobia are intertwined concepts" (Gaard 2011, 1). Serenella Iovino uses the term "sexophobia" and links it with ecophobia (see Iovino 2013, 44).

[29] All citations of Shakespeare's works in this study are from *The Riverside Shakespeare, 2nd Edition* (1997).

Read notes that the early modern midwife Jane Sharp draws a linguistic parallel between the words "menstruous" and "monstrous" (see Sharp 1999, 215) and argues that this is but the tip of a much larger obsession with vilifying the liquid materialities of women's bodies – materialities that center on and extend from the vagina. Lear is hardly peculiar in his time for conceptualizing the vagina as a place of stench, consumption, and leakage.

The image of Woman as a leaky vessel has long been a dominant sexist standpoint. Gail Kern Paster explains that "the weaker vessel [. . . is the] leaky vessel" (Paster 1993, 24) in early modern thinking and that

> this discourse inscribes women as leaky vessels by isolating one element of the female body's material expressiveness – its production of fluids – as excessive, hence either disturbing or shameful. It also characteristically links this liquid expressiveness to excessive verbal fluency. In both formations, the issue is women's bodily self-control or, more precisely, the representation of a particular kind of uncontrol as a function of gender. (25)

While clearly one of the issues here has to do with the imagined threat of "uncontrolled" female agency (verbal and sexual), there is also something else going on. Drawing on a treatise published in 1601 by essayist Pierre Charron (one of the disciples of Montaigne), Sophie Chiari maintains that "with their vapours, humours, and fluids, men and women's bodies were [. . .] comparable to small, independent weather systems. Human passions were liquids saturating the body and in need of control, a little like torrential rains threatening to flood the land" (Chiari 2019, 15). This is an insight with profound implications, since if bodies are weather systems writ small, then weather systems are bodies writ large. What this means is that weather systems (and, by implication, climate) are gendered. Moreover, the fluids we are talking about from "the leaky vessel" here are not waters from clean mountain streams: in the early modern male imagination, the vagina is a place of fluids and slimes that cause corruption, decay, and poisoning,[30] a place of rot that provokes fear and disgust among men, with nothing less than biblical authority promoting the idea.[31] It is perhaps, therefore, something of an understatement to claim that "there was a degree of animosity towards the vagina in the early modern period" (Alberti).[32]

---

[30] See also Read, who offers meticulous discussions of the early modern notion that menstrual blood and excretions were corrupting and poisonous (see, in particular, 24–38).

[31] See *Isaiah* 64.6 (64.5 in the original Hebrew text). There are different translations of the original, some mentioning menstrual rags, others not. The *Common English Bible* translates וַנְּהִי כַטָּמֵא כֻּלָּנוּ, וּכְבֶגֶד עִדִּים כָּל-צִדְקֹתֵינוּ as "all our righteous deeds are like a menstrual rag," while *The New International Version* offers "all our righteous acts are like filthy rags" and the *King James Bible* "all our righteousnesses are as filthy rags." There is no mention of menstruation or blood in the Hebrew original.

[32] This paragraph appears in an earlier form in Estok 2023b.

Reviewing misogynist traditions expressed in Swift, Milton, and Sartre, Camille Paglia describes the "squalid womb-world" and "mucoid swamp" of "fishy female jellies" as the "road to Lear's hell" (Paglia 1990, 94). Notwithstanding her horrendous mixing of metaphors, Paglia has an important point: there is a long tradition associating women with slime, disgust, and corporeal menace and threat. In literary and scientific discussions of slime, as Wedlich has argued, stigmatization of entire groups of people has been common, and "a long and inglorious tradition has seen women forced into this category – as the apparently slimier sex" (Wedlich 2021, 9). Central to this stigmatization is a gendered disgust that historically resembles Lear's. Wedlich is clearly aware, however, of the ambivalence of this slimic disgust. The exploration on the topic from Martha Nussbaum's *Washington Post* article is compelling and well worth quoting at length here for how it encapsulates this ambivalence:

> Disgust for women's bodily fluids is fully compatible with sexual desire. Indeed, it often singles out women seen as promiscuous, the repositories of many men's fluids. [...] As the great philosopher Adam Smith observed about post-coital disgust, "When we have dined, we order the covers to be removed." Disgust for the female body is always tinged with anxiety, since the body symbolizes mortality. Disgust is often more deeply buried than envy and anger, but it compounds and intensifies the other negative emotions. Our president [Mr. Trump] seems to be especially gripped by disgust: for women's menstrual fluids, their bathroom breaks, the blood imagined streaming from their surgical incisions, even their flesh, if they are more than stick-thin. (Nussbaum 2018)

Nussbaum's comments are important because of the frightening frequency with which people turn a blind eye to powerful men and their myxophobic misogyny. If it is tempting to be an apologist for Shakespeare and the misogyny he stages, or for supporting fans to laugh off the sexist antics, actions, and comments of Mr. Trump, so, too, has it proven irresistible to exonerate Sartre. He has, after all, contributed a lot to the theorizing of slime and has productively advocated an antisexist philosophy.

2.2 Sartre

Despite their breathtaking originality, Sartre's comments on slime entirely ignore the gendering of slime, much of it his own. Sartre's gender "silence" has not gone unnoticed, and he has been called down for not only missing the chance to comment upon gender but of himself articulating sexist positions in his comments on slime. Constance Mui, for instance, argues that there is "unmistakably sexist language in Sartre's discussions of the slimy and the hole, which he associates with the breast and the vagina, organs that are distinctively female" (Mui 1990, 31).

Whether or not Sartre is, as Mui claims in an *ad hominem* attack,[33] a "grumbling misogynist" (31), the language of *Being and Nothingness* is clearly damning. Hazel Barnes has put it well: "There can be no doubt that a full investigation of the linguistic codes in Sartre's writing would reveal him to be a man comfortably ensconced in a world of male dominance" (Barnes 1990, 341), but Barnes, like Margery Collins and Christine Pierce (whose pioneering "Holes and Slime: Sexism in Sartre's Psychoanalysis" made the first claim about sexist language in *Being and Nothingness*), and like Mui also, suggests that the sexist contingencies of the language "are [weaknesses that are] at variance with the central philosophy" of the text itself (Barnes 1990, 341). Mui ironically defends Sartrean philosophy as essentially antisexist (ironic because she does so at least in part through an *ad hominem* attack): "One cannot infer from the sexist analogies of slime and holes the claim that woman occupies an inferior ontological status. To do so would be to overlook the delightful irony in his ontology: in spite of his ill feelings toward woman, woman nevertheless prevails as a full-fledged consciousness in that ontology" (Mui 1990, 32).

Yet, it is neither what he does in his personal life with women nor his antisexist postures in various parts of *Being and Nothingness* that is at issue here: what is at issue are his sexist comments about slime. The cherry-picking by scholars seeking to exonerate Sartre of sexism results in pure nonsense. It is sham scholarship to say "X pleases me but Y – even though it contradicts X – is irrelevant." To call Sartre's sexist comments "contingencies of language" is to miss the point entirely, rather like saying that rape and clitorectomies are contingencies of culture. Sadly, this kind of exoneration is what Sartre apologists argue for. Better to get on with it. Better to acknowledge that he clearly wants to support a feminist position but is equally clearly unable to do so. Slime "is like a leech sucking me" (Sartre 1966, 773), Sartre explains, adding that "it is a soft, yielding action, a moist and feminine sucking" (776). Woman as leech? This is sexism enough, but he goes on. Having associated slime with "feminine sucking," he then associates it with "the possessed [. . .] dog" (776), "a poisonous possession" (776), a "snare" (776), "a sickly-sweet feminine revenge" (777), and a "sugary death" (777). Implicitly, these are all a part of the feminine sucking that slime is for him. The images Sartre uses in association with women – feminine sucking, possessed dog, revenge, and death – are deeply

---

[33] It seems hard to separate the personal from the professional (or, to be more precise in this case, from the professed). Wedlich cites Sarah Bakewell's theory that "Sartre, if we can judge by the vivid descriptions in his books, found sex a nightmarish process of struggling not to drown in slime and gloop" (Wedlich 2021, 24). Even so, Sartre's failure to understand the gendering of slime (in which he participated) has significantly hindered the very theorizing about slime he sought to promote.

misogynistic. Perhaps it is possible to write off Lear's vaginophobia, just as it is possible to dismiss Sartre's or Trump's sexism, as a contingency, but both actions are counter-productive and are clearly not in the interests of feminism – or the environment.

To fully understand the environmental implications of a slime-based sexism (or a myxophobic misogyny), understanding the long history of slime's gendering (culminating in a giant such as Jean-Paul Sartre) is necessary. The apparent myxophobic misogyny of Sartre's work is certainly enmeshed with patriarchal ideologies that find popular expression (in films, for instance) that potentially reaches millions.

2.3 Alien Mother

Perhaps no recent text reveals the conceptualization of gendered slime quite as well as the *Alien* franchise, which began with Ridley Scott's 1979 *Alien*. The films feature a near-perfect parasitic extraterrestrial species capable of surviving virtually any trauma or environment and driven by fierce compulsions to reproduce and survive. Center stage are the female aliens that, near-perfect though the species may be, have slime constantly dripping from their mouths. It seems improbable that such a species would slaver like a common mutt, but slime – perhaps because of the disgust it evokes[34] – is a central conceit of the horror genre. And clearly, it is not just slime and disgust that evoke horror here. Gender is involved. The alien is female, her opponent is female (Warrant officer Ellen Ripley, played by Sigourney Weaver), and the ship's computer is called "Mother." There is a case to be made that the film empowers women, to be sure, but it is not a compelling or convincing case. In a brilliant discussion of the topic, Judith Newton explains that "the most obviously utopian element in *Alien* is its casting of a female character in the role of individualist hero, a role conventionally played by a male" (Newton 1990, 82). Certainly, the hero of the film is a woman: Ripley, believe it or not. Newton demonstrates that

> the film expresses two fantasies. The first is that individual action has resolved economic and social horrors, for all the anxieties which the film evokes about the de-humanizing force of late-capitalist labour have been deflected onto the alien. The second fantasy is that white, middle-class women, once integrated into the world of work, will somehow save us from its worst excesses and specifically from its dehumanization. (83)

---

[34] Like Noël Carroll, William Ian Miller sees a close connection between disgust and horror. He explains in *The Anatomy of Disgust*, "horror is a subset of disgust, being specifically that disgust for which no distancing or evasive strategies exist that are not in themselves utterly contaminating" (Miller 1997, 26). Similarly, Carolyn Korsmeyer and Barry Smith maintain that "fear, contempt, horror, [and] loathing" are kin to disgust (Korsmeyer and Smith 2004, 2).

But there is a more immediate seemingly feminist element of this film: "What *Alien* offers on one level, and to a white, middle-class audience, is a utopian fantasy of women's liberation, a fantasy of economic and social equality, friendship and collectivity between middle-class women and men" (84). So, then, where does this leave black women or Asian women or women from the Global South? Moreover, Newton is acutely aware that the film poses but does not deliver on its feminist potentials. Newton goes on to discuss various misogynistic images of the alien's agency, egg-laying, "womb-like and vagina-like spaces" (85), "vaginal teeth" (85), the various victories Ash has over Ripley, and so on to show that the film really does not do much for women – and even less so when we consider the gender implications of slime. Slime, however, does not slither into Newton's discussion. Other theorists have discussed women, gender, and sexism in the *Alien* franchise (see, for instance, Bell-Metereau 1985; Rushing 1989; Kavanagh 1990; Vaughn 1995; Davis 2000; Doherty 2015), but slime does not ooze into these discussions either.

The slime dripping from the alien's mouth is clearly not some evolutionary function Ridley Scott imagines, but an ideological one. There will be female-on-female fighting (known in sexist and speciesist vernacular as "catfights"). The sexualized violence here that takes its meaning through the female body that the narrative objectifies but does not empower. Any empowerment the film affords women (as hero) quickly dissipates when the main protagonist appears in skimpy underwear, and given that she is fighting a drooling "bitch" – the teaser trailer for *Alien 3* states "the bitch is back" (see *Alien 3*, 1992) – the stakes are clearly mapped out on the female body. Ripley is the sexy dominatrix, objectified and therefore controlled, her body the site through which this control is managed, and it is a body threatened by a less pretty, less sexy mother figure – who happens to be slavering slime.

By the time Ripley has become genetically infected in the franchise with the genes of the "bitch," the specter of monstrosity looms. The now not-so-exceptional human sits at the contested definitional axes of the natural body, a kiss away from monstrosity. We witness here how, as Judith Butler explains, "the construction of the human is a differential operation that produces the more and the less 'human,' the inhuman, the humanly unthinkable. These excluded sites come to bound the 'human' as its constitutive outside, and to haunt those boundaries as the persistent possibility of their disruption and rearticulation" (Butler 1993, 8). Writing monstrosity is the narrativization of ecophobia, the imagining of unpredictable agency in nature that must be subject to human power and discipline. Ecophobia is the disciplinary reaction, and it is all about power.

It is the something-other-than-humanness that is dangerous in the monster, and in order for this danger to have any potency, we need a conception of the other-than-human as hostile, malevolent. When Kelly Hurley explains that "slime is the revenge of matter, which seeks to swallow up the known and bounded world into its own amorphousness" (Hurley 1996, 38), we approach the slimy core of the matter, so to speak, or the core of slimy matter. Hurley continues: "In slime, matter displays itself in all its ineluctability. As an anomalous phenomenon, slime testifies to the inability of human classificatory systems to contain and master matter; as a tactile experience, sliminess is a reminder of the utter Thing-ness of matter. From here it is a short step to positing matter as somehow malevolent" (36). And positing matter as somehow malevolent is ecophobia writ large – and slime is central here.

The slimic is evil just *because* it is slimic, as the Jew to the anti-Semite is vile for no other reason that he or she is a Jew, as the African-American is inferior to the racist for no other reason that he or she is black, and as the natural is threatening for no other reason that it (often gendered "she") is the natural. It is in the potential agency of each that the threat lies – and there are intimate links among these maladaptive phobic responses. Gendering slime and colocating the disgust it produces with women is dangerously sexist. When men see women as sites of pollution, what Mary Douglas calls "matter out of place" (Douglas 1984, 36), effectively they see women as matter that they can control and rearrange and that they can put right and clean up. Slime, a shape-shifter that defies categories, triggers ecophobic disgust precisely because of the threat it poses to human order, and while we should make no mistake about it that it is a *male* order,[35] we also need to understand that there is much more to it than that.

2.4 Class and Race

There's a thousand ways to rationalize a racist. (Michael 2016)

Rationalizing racism often resembles the kinds of apologist remarks about Sartre and Shakespeare we have seen. Graham Harman famously rationalizes H.P. Lovecraft's very well-documented racism, explaining that "in certain rare cases, reactionary views might improve the power of an imaginative writer [. . . and] that Lovecraft's racism may be such a case" (Harman 2012, 59). In a letter to Frank Belknap Long, Lovecraft describes Manhattan's Lower East Side as follows:

---

[35] How men imagine the agency of women – sexual, emotional, intellectual, political (and how they fear what they imagine) – is inseparable from the physical workings of bodies, and in the case of sexual agency and women's arousal, what are the implications of the intersections between fear and contempt of slime, on the one hand, and misogyny and violence on the other? What happens when patriarchies imagine women, women's bodies, and women's sexuality as sites of pollution articulated through slimic discourses? What is the rendering of the agential female body in the patriarchal imagination, and is FGM (female genital mutilation) the result?

The organic things – Italo-Semitico-Mongoloid – inhabiting that awful cess-pool could not by any stretch of the imagination be call'd human. They were monstrous and nebulous adumbrations of the pithecanthropoid and amoebal; vaguely moulded from some stinking viscous slime of earth's corruption, and slithering and oozing in and on the filthy streets or in and out of windows and doorways in a fashion suggestive of nothing but infesting worms or deep-sea unnamabilities. They – or the degenerate gelatinous fermentation of which they were composed – seem'd to ooze, seep and trickle thro' the gaping cracks in the horrible houses … and I thought of some avenue of Cyclopean and unwholesome vats, crammed to the vomiting-point with gangrenous vileness, and about to burst and innundate the world in one leprous cataclysm of semi-fluid rottenness. (Cited in Houellebecq 2005, 106–107)

Despite Harman's rationalizations, this is in-your-face racism, and it is certainly slimic. Philip Roth's representations of slime's entanglements with race, class, and ethnicity are decidedly more sophisticated, nuanced, and understated.

A pivotal scene in Roth's *Nemesis* (2010) involves a swath of slime that importantly, if subtly, demonstrates mutual involvements of gender, race, and class with the slimic imagination and elemental eco-horror. A group of young Italian hoodlums have arrived in the Jewish neighborhood looking for trouble. When the novel's central protagonist Bucky Cantor asks them why they have come to the neighborhood, "'We're spreadin' polio,' one of the Italians replied." Class and ethnicity are tightly stitched into the fabric of the narrative here. The Italians have come from the East Side, which was "the industrial slum," an area "that had reported the most cases of polio so far" in the narrative (Roth 2010, 13).

The environmental justice movement addresses this issue and calls "attention to the ways disparate distribution of wealth and power often leads to [. . .] the unequal distribution of environmental degradation and/or toxicity" (Adamson, Evans, and Stein 2002, 5). Environmental justice scholars have made clear and irrefutable "connections between race, class, and environmental ills, amassing strong evidence that communities of color and communities of the poor suffer far more from such problems than do whiter wealthier communities" (2). Clearly, however, it is also gendered violence that is implied in the *Nemesis* spitting scene. It is a gendered scene not only because it is men being violent but because of the kind of violence they are enacting – namely, forcing themselves on their mostly passive victims. Cantor walks up to them and stands his ground, but the scene reaches a kind of climax despite this resistance. The hoodlums spit and then casually leave. What remains are the slimy remnants of the climax: "It turned out that there was sputum spread over the wide area of pavement where the Italian guys had congregated, some twenty feet of a wet, slimy, disgusting mess that certainly appeared an ideal breeding ground for the disease" (Roth 2010, 16). The isomorphic tags of rape here are unmistakable, and the monstrous birth that will result from this metaphorical crime is the materialization of the disease, though the narrative does not pronounce a verdict.[36] On the contrary, the narrative diffuses the source of engenderment, with characters arguing about the situation:

> "It had to be the Italians."
> "No, no, I don't think so. I was there when the Italians came. They had no contact with the children. It wasn't the Italians." (38)

Later, race and ethnicity remain central, as the source of the engenderment remains a mystery:

> The anti-Semites are saying that it's because they're Jews that polio spreads there. Because of all the Jews – that's why Weequahic is the center of the paralysis and why the Jews should be isolated. Some of them sound as if they think the best way to get rid of the polio epidemic would be to burn down Weequahic with all the Jews in it. (193)

References to "the day the Italians tried to invade the playground" (62) continue throughout the novel, slime taking center stage. The subtlety and ambivalence of slime are evident here, and it is clear that race, class, and gender are involved with this strange element that Brayton describes as "a material condition that is neither chemical nor biological in nature, but fundamentally liminal and marginal – between solid and liquid, inert and alive" (Brayton 2015, 81). It is worth mentioning, too, that racism and sexism are clearly implied in Jack Arnold's 1954 horror classic *Creature from the Black Lagoon*. Part of the threat of corruption from the slimy monster in this film is that it is foreign, a monster from the shallows of a lagoon in the depths of the Amazon jungle. "Gill-man," as the creature is called, is not from Seattle. He is a monster from abroad, a monster because he bears human form but clearly is not human, a monster because he breathes both in and out of water, a monster—worst of all and most threateningly—because he has his horny little eyes set on a helpless white woman, which, of course, plays into a long tradition of sexism and xenophobia. Conceptually, slime is indeed deeply entangled with fears about threats to human integrity, and in America, "human" has often meant white, male, and middle-class. It has also meant heterosexual.

3 Entanglements

3.1 Queer Little Nightmares

Slime is queer. It is an element that calls into question virtually all of the boundaries that we live by. It is an element that troubles the living with the

---

[36] Although the victims of this violence are also male, there is a long tradition that "feminizes" Jewish men. For an interesting discussion of this matter, see Boyarin 1995.

dead,[37] the fully constituted subject from the abject and the nonhuman, the acceptable from the taboo, and the edible from the disgusting. In an edited collection entitled *Queer Little Nightmares: An Anthology of Monstrous Fiction and Poetry*,[38] the Japanese-Canadian writer Hiromi Goto shockingly exposes these slimic unsettlings in her short story "And the Moon Spun Round Like a Top." Bernadette Nakashima, the central protagonist, is approaching menopause and has "big blood clots" during her menstrual period which, after going online, she discovers "was normal [. . .] during 'the change'" (Goto 2022, 121). One of these clots was "the size of a hamster" and "almost looked like one, with four stubby, limb-like protrusions [and a] rounded bulge that was almost a head . . ." (121). It had a "jelly-like consistency" (121). Then she finds that it is alive: it "recoiled from her touch" and then "humped and squirmed, humped and squirmed like a plump red grub on the sticky surface of her gusset" (121). Then another one came out, "a hot, round bulge [that] billowed through her vagina [. . .] slid out, slick and easy" (124). As she is trying to make sense of it all, "the giant clot of blood squealed" and "continued shrieking – a piercing pitch" followed finally by "a quiet mewing" (125).[39] Moments later when she is holding the thing, it starts sucking her blood: "A sharp pain punched through her forefinger, the fleshy part below the first joint. Bernadette gasped. Sucking. She could feel the suction, the painful throb of her broken flesh. The wet sounds of swallowing" (125). She wonders, "What manner of life was this?" (125). What manner indeed! Barbara Creed has noted in her discussions of Julia Kristeva's work that "the ultimate in abjection is the corpse" and in order to avoid becoming a corpse, "the body protects itself from bodily wastes, such as shit, blood, urine and pus by ejecting these things from the body just as it expels food that, for whatever reason, the subject finds loathesome" (Creed 1993, 9). She explains that "slime, bile, pus, vomit, urine, [and] blood [are all . . .] abject forms of excrement" (40). The slimy thing that has come out of Bernadette's vagina, as it turns out, is neither bodily waste nor an abject form of excrement. It is a living thing, and she suckles it with her blood.[40] It is apparently also intelligent. It stops making noise when Timo, the caretaker of the building, comes up to see if everything is all right. He is satisfied that it is, but clearly it is

---

[37] My wording here is inspired by Mel Y. Chen's comment in *Animacies: Biopolitics, Racial Mattering, and Queer Affect* that "contemporary biopolitics is [. . .] troubling the living with the dead" (Chen 2012, 6)

[38] I am grateful to graduate student Annabella Emilia Nemeth for bringing this collection to my attention.

[39] This is reminiscent of "the slime in the pit [that] seemed to utter cries and voices" in *Dr. Jeckyll and Mr. Hyde* (Stevenson 2003, 60) that I referenced in Section 1.2.

[40] This clearly flouts the biblical dietary prohibition of mixing blood and milk (Exodus 23:19, 34:26, Deuteronomy 14:21). See also Kristeva 1982, 105.

not. This slimic monstrosity "had no face. No eyes. And yet it had a mouth for eating. Teeth for biting" (Goto 2022, 126). Clearly a very aggressive version of the vagina dentata trope, these slimy blood clots multiply, and Bernadette "could not say how many skinless creatures she had passed during the long night" (128). She collected them all in "jars, soup pots, bowls, . . . basins, a cat carrier, some old Tupperware containers and, of all things, a discarded baby's bathtub" (128), and then when the officious caretaker returns (this time because he thinks that the noises he hears are pets), we get horror, pure horror: "*Thud. Thud. Clatter.* Things falling from a height. *Bang, bang, bang.* Like someone kicking the kitchen cupboards with a workboot" (130). The slime clots ate him.[41] Moreover, Bernadette had given so much of herself to make these creatures – "the entire day spent bleeding creatures into the tub" (130) – that she herself was starved, and "the sounds of crunching bones, slurping and sucking, made [her] stomach rumble. Juices filled her mouth" (130). Before long, "the hunger in her belly roared," and as "the creatures surged around her, [. . .] she grabbed them, the little ones falling into the back of her mouth like raw oysters. *Plip, plop, plip*" (135).[42] She drew before her "a writhing, shimmering mound" and "gulped and gulped like a starving sea turtle eating an entire ocean of jellyfish" (135). Clearly, there is *a lot* going on in this story with slime.

The first and most obvious slimic issue in this narrative is the subversion of hetero-reproductive norms. Bernadette is producing life without a man: "she hadn't had sex for over nine years" (122). According to Bernadette's friend, Glenda, "who referred to herself as queer" (119), Bernadette herself is also queer: "even though she might not be gay," Glenda says, "jeez was she ever queer" (119). Bernadette's "walk around Lost Lagoon at Stanley Park" (115) in Vancouver only adds to this unspoken fact. Lost Lagoon is a famous gay cruising area in Vancouver (admittedly more for men than for women, but still it is a queer zone). It is clear that she does not need or want men, and the life she makes without a man is one that she suckles with her own blood

---

[41] Goto is clearly toying with what Creed describes as "male fears and phantasies about the female genitals as a trap, a black hole which threatens to swallow them up and cut them into pieces" (Creed 1993, 106). Creed explains the deep classical roots of the vagina dentata trope and notes that "the notion of the devouring female genitals continues to exist in the modern world; it is apparent in popular derogatory terms such as 'man-eater' and 'castrating bitch'" (106). Goto's version of the vagina with teeth is less passive than traditional images of castrating female genitals: indeed, this man-eater entirely disengages from the vagina and goes out into the world, focusing not on the prized penis but the entire man. Good-bye Timo!

[42] It is perhaps worth observing here that patriarchies have long viewed oysters as an aphrodisiac. This scene thus evokes images both of cunnilingus and of cannibalism – the latter both because Bernadette ends up eating her own offspring and because they eat her: "*Cannibal,* she thought. *My body . . . part of me . . . is a cannibal*" (127).

(perhaps raising the issue of how this story re-articulates questions about the lesbian vampire genre).[43]

The centrality of menstrual blood in this story forces a focus on a slimic material coded in patriarchal texts as a defilement, as excrement, as stuff not to be regarded. Goto actively resists such a demonizing of menstrual blood. Not only is it central to this story; it is also ultimately ingested, becoming sustenance rather than poisonous impurity, life-affirming rather than mortal in effect, hardly the threat it is for men. Julia Kristeva shows how "menstrual blood [...] threatens the relationship between the sexes within a social aggregate and, through internalization, the identity of each sex in the face of sexual difference" (Kristeva 1982, 71); however, life, this story suggests, is simply not what patriarchies portray it as. Eagerly anticipating her next period, Bernadette muses on everything: "Oh, remarkable life ... Every cell in her body sang" (Goto 2022, 136). Goto expresses the "potentials of queer becoming shaped by [...] aqueous entanglements," to borrow a phrase out-of-context from Jeremy Chow (Chow 2023, 4). Bernadette subverts slime's registers and everything that Kristeva says about menstrual blood as a sign of abjection. Kristeva writes that

> Excrement and its equivalents (decay, infection, disease, corpse, etc.) stand for the danger to identity that comes from without: the ego threatened by the non-ego, society threatened by its outside, life by death. Menstrual blood, on the contrary, stands for the danger issuing from within the identity (social or sexual). (Kristeva 1982, 71)

But in Goto, menstrual blood and slime are not the threat of life by death.

3.2 Life

> Ultimately, is sliminess not the sacred, the taboo substance of life itself? (Morton 2007, 159)

Our relationship with the waters of our planet is well known, and, as Astrida Neimanis so cogently explains, "our own embodiment [...] is never really autonomous":

> We are literally implicated in other animal, vegetable, and planetary bodies that materially course through us, replenish us, and draw upon our own

---

[43] In *Vampires and Violets*, Emmy Award winning filmmaker Andrea Weiss reports that "the lesbian vampire is the most persistent lesbian image in the history of cinema" (Weiss 1992, 84) but that "the typical lesbian vampire film, belonging within the horror/exploitation genre, is an articulation of men's subconscious fear of and hostility toward women's sexuality" (103). She also claims that in these films, "the vampire's thirst for blood and the association of blood with menstruation makes mocking reference to female life-giving capacities, inverting them into life-taking ones" (103). Goto clearly does her own inversion of the patriarchal "lesbian vampire" trope, her "vampire" producing life (and then eating it!).

bodies as their wells: human bodies ingest reservoir bodies, while reservoir bodies are slaked by rain bodies, rain bodies absorb ocean bodies, ocean bodies aspirate fish bodies, fish bodies are consumed by whale bodies – which then sink to the seafloor to rot and be swallowed up again by the ocean's dark belly. (Neimanis 2017, 3)

Neimanis notes that "as bodies of porosity, we are constantly interpermeating our surroundings" (76).[44] She describes how

Our watery bodies can serve as the soupy gestational matter for our material passions and can invite a mingling of these passions in such a way that the discreteness of our individualized bodies begins to dissolve. While we can leak beyond the boundaries of our molar bodies, this transubstantiation of bodies into viscous ooze is also a marker of the mingling of our bodies with those potential bodies of water that we have incorporated – those fishy, watery beginnings that we carry with us as material, vestigial potentiality. (138)

For instance, during sex, she explains, citing Alphonso Lingis, "our muscular and vertebrate bodies transubstantiate into ooze, slime, mammalian sweat, and reptilian secretions, into minute tadpoles and releases of hot moist breath nourishing the floating microorganisms of the night air" (Lingis 2000, 38, as cited by Neimanis 2017, 138). Neimanis is also clear that "phallogocentrism, the masculinist logic of sharp-edged self-sufficiency [. . .] supports a forgetting of the bodies that have gestated our own" (3) – which, effectively, is both a misogynistic revulsion toward the corporeality of women and a variety of myxophobia.

Slime is complex, entangled with life as much as with death. Life begins in slime. Lorenz Oken notes "that all organic beings originate from [. . .] the unfusorial mass, or the protoplasm [*Urschleim*] from whence all larger organisms fashion themselves or are evolved. Their production is therefore nothing else than a regular agglomeration of [. . .] mucus vesicles or points [*Schleimpunkte*], which first form themselves by their union or combination into particular species" (Oken 1847/2015, xi–xii). People who eat eggs see this slime in the yolk and the whites, and horror is perhaps the result when there is a bloody little embryo in the mix.

Even in its associations with life, slime can ambivalently embody horror – and not only in unwanted embryos. In *Pilgrim at Tinker Creek*, for instance, Annie Dillard is in pure awe at the baffling fecundity of the natural world. Early in Chapter 10, she recalls a nightmare she had wherein she had witnessed two giant Luna moths mating,

---

[44] Melody Jue similarly talks of "the porosity of embodiment" (Jue 2020,19).

And then the eggs hatched and the bed was full of fish. I was standing across the room in the doorway, staring at the bed. The eggs hatched before my eyes, on my bed, and a thousand chunky fish swarmed there in a viscid slime. The fish were firm and fat, black and white, with triangular bodies and bulging eyes. I watched in horror as they squirmed three feet deep, swimming and oozing about in the glistening, transparent slime. Fish in the bed! (Dillard 1985, 160)

And then she awoke screaming. The horror of things out of place—such as fish in the bed!—is only a part of the nightmare, the larger part being unwelcome slime in it. Moreover, when such a thing as slime generates life and agency, it adds to the horror, since we harbor a deep cognitive resistance to the notion of agency within something as cellularly heterogenous as slime.

Undoubtedly, another reason for the horror is the very lack of diversity slime seems to represent. On some visceral level, and I expect that we will eventually find biological evidence for this, it seems that we are repulsed by too much uniformity and are threatened by ideas about the loss of diversity. Perhaps this is part of the reason why the marching armies of enemy countries seem so frightening. It has to do with loss of individuality and identity, and Allison Mackey seems correct in maintaining that "the fear and mistrusts of the fungal stems at least in part from the terror of losing one's own individuality by merging into a collective entity" (Mackey 2023, 253). So, too, with slime and its mono-cellularity. It is not simply that the appearance of slimy creatures such as jellyfish often "confus[e] the categories of solidity and liquidity," as Stacy Alaimo has pointed out (Alaimo 2013, 145) but that such creatures, like slime itself, inspires an "ontological confusion and panic" (152). Alaimo goes on to argue that "gelata, ever so gently, question the humanist desire for solid demarcations" (154) and "float at the far reaches of our ability to construct sturdy interspecies connections, thus posing both conceptual and ethical challenges" (140). And of all the connections slime troubles, that between life and death is perhaps most disturbing.

3.3 Death and the Undead

Slime and death are inseparable. The association of slime with the trope of disintegration is very present in VanderMeer's *Annihilation*, and as "the path of slime grew thicker" (VanderMeer 2014, 58), the narrator's fear of disintegration increased. Her husband, who had always been "outgoing and impetuous and [. . .] passionate" came back from the previous expedition to the slimy tunnel with "none of that in him" (57). Life, as it were, has been sucked from him.

Annihilation is a part of a growing body of what has come to be known as fungal fiction, and, predictably, it is a genre in which slime is central. Fungal fiction is a subgenre of ecohorror that embodies our worst fears. According to

Evelyn Koch, "fungal fiction represents our human fears of global infections, decay, and ultimately extinction" (Koch 2023, 280). While fungi are essential to life, "it is," Koch explains, "the darker side of fungi that unsettles us: their ability to feast on death to form new life" (279). Yet, slime settles on both life and death. It is the "agony of water," but it is not water.

Slime is a shape-shifter, an amorphous thing that differs from water in how it characterizes the bodies and things it touches. It invests them with ethically charged identities. Water just makes things wet; slime makes them disgusting or horrifying or dangerous. Water dries; slime infects. Water takes the speediest route; slime is in no rush. Slime twists and turns the concept of spatial integrity and invests it with a multiplicity of potentials for inhabitation and reinhabitation. Slime is radical in this sense. It collapses capitalist ideals about the management of space and in turn the management of time too. A critique of these ideals takes clear form in the insatiable, unsustainable, and mindless hunger of the slimy zombies that populate the television adaptation of Robert Kirkman's comic book series *The Walking Dead*.

The apocalypse begins in a French science laboratory, on one of the walls of which hangs a slogan reading "Les Morts Sont Nés Ici" ("The dead are born here"). The series suggests that it is unimportant both what the exact purpose of the viral research was or how the virus got out (it seems to have been unintentional); what is important is that the zombie apocalypse is the result of human fiddlings with genes and viruses. The critique of medical and military institutions, however, is the very tip of the iceberg here, and this is not just some ridiculous comic book fantasy. The science behind it all is perhaps even plausible, argues clinical microbiologist Anisha Misra (see Misra 2023). Whether or not this is so, the fictional virus is airborne, and no one is immune. Everyone carries it. When they die, the virus slows decomposition and reactivates the brain stem allowing only the basic survival instincts to work – and, incidentally, these are ones that tend not to show humanity in its best light. The zombies engage in mindless cannibalism of the living, who then "turn" and do the same. Civilization totally breaks down. As civilization collapses, the remnants of our world struggle both against the zombie enemy (called "the walkers" in the series) and against each other. The horror of the zombie enemy would be very different without the slime. These creatures are dead and rotting, their slime infectious, like the saliva of The Komodo Dragon.[45] The slimy borders of these walkers challenge and dissolve the boundary between the living and the dead – a challenge neatly congealed in the oxymoronic title of the series. Spaces

---

[45] Komodo Dragons are living dinosaurs that can reach up to three meters and seventy kilograms. The bacteria in the slime of their saliva is thought to be more dangerous than their actual bite and to be the cause of the death of most of their prey.

mortal to the human frame are inhabitable to these zombies. They challenge the understandings of space and protocols about corporeality. The walking dead demand a total recalibration of physical responses to human bodies, a need for astonishing and widespread violence against the integrity of the living dead that inhabit the deliquescent human frame.

Even without the deliquescence, the trope of the zombie alone is a strong figure of resistance. Laura Wright explains why zombies serve as an excellent vehicle of social critique: "zombies have consistently lacked the ability to reason; they are driven by a thoughtless and amoral consumption and have served as ideal metaphors for an increasingly consumer-based culture that is often driven by unethical production models" (Wright 2015, 69). These unethical production models take full form in *The Walking Dead* among the still-living groups that use weapons, extortion, totalitarianism, and so on to battle each other for control of resources and power. The battle is as much against what animates the live human frame as the dead, a battle as much against the human survival instincts that pit us against each other as against the threat of degeneration that the waves of slimic zombies represent. The threat of death and degeneration that slime poses is perhaps a part of the ecophobic vision of the return of Nature (about which I wrote in *The Ecophobia Hypothesis*, 66).

3.4 Ecophobia and Slime

Ecophobia is central to promoting the sense of human particularity – corporeal, intellectual, and spiritual – that has enabled incredible accomplishments for our species. Our porous corporeality is fundamental here, and as locus, gauge, and conduit for both our self-assurance and our fears, the body is the site through which ecophobia takes meaning and expression. Resisting ecophobic impulses means moving away from the sense of particularity and exceptionalism we maintain, away "from the entrenched notion of humanity's privileged status as if it exists outside of earth systems" (Oppermann 2017, 143–44). One of the ways to achieve this movement away from the sense of self-entitlement and exceptionalism is, as Stacy Alaimo has put it, by "thinking across bodies." So doing "may catalyze the recognition that the environment, which is too often imagined as inert, empty space or as a resource for human use, is, in fact, a world of fleshy beings with their own needs, claims, and actions" (Alaimo 2010, 2). It is precisely such agency and the intimacy of the threats it offers that often evokes the maladaptive response of ecophobia, and perhaps nowhere is this more evident than in our complicated responses to rot and slime – significant at least in part because these responses are a disturbing playground of ecophobia.

We have good reason to fear dirty and rotting things: they have not promoted our well-being in our evolutionary history. No one would call it ecophobic to avoid mortality and shun bacterial and viral threats. Bacteria in film and literature rarely offers an accurate understanding of bacteria and is more often than not phobic in its representations. In the 2004 romantic comedy *Along Came Polly*, for instance, Reuben Feffer (played by Ben Stiller) explains to Polly Prince (played by Jennifer Aniston) that "when you think you're innocently eating a little bar snack, you're actually ingesting potentially deadly bacteria from about 39 soil-handed strangers. I mean, people wonder why they get E. coli poisoning or salmonella or hepatitis, when all they gotta do is look at the snack bowl at their local watering hole. . . .It's an absolute hot zone in there." Feffer's fears border on the phobic.

Post-pandemic compulsive use of hand sanitizers in public venues (and I confess to have sanitized as much as, and perhaps more than, anyone else) is a recent example of our further trek down the road of obsessive fear of dirt and bacteria. The reality, however (and this is not to take the idiotic position of the antivaxxers), is that the human body is comprised of more nonhuman than human DNA, and *obsessive* hand sanitizing is more harmful in the long run than it is beneficial in that we are killing microorganisms that are beneficial to our own survival. For instance, we need intestinal flora in order to digest our food, regulate our immune system, and reduce inflammation. These gut flora (the bacteria) produce antimicrobial substances that outnumber the total count of cells in the human body by 1,000 percent–ten to one, in other words. The biological questions about what we are doing to future generations with our compulsive sanitizing need our attention. No less does our sense of being besieged, outnumbered, and under attack by our microscopic companions need attention; imagining war rather than cohabitation with the microbes will not help us in the long run, and the fact remains that "we are more microbe than human" (McFall-Ngai 2017, M52). There will be consequences for tearing into microbial ecosystems.

We are facing a serious loss – one that has nothing to do with personal liberties or social freedoms. Before COVID-19, with the growth of the Anthropocene, we had already begun to face "the loss," Margaret McFall-Ngai explains, "of the complex microbial worlds both within and beyond organismal bodies – worlds that make nearly all life possible" (M51). These microbial worlds are absolutely essential for us, yet we are tearing into them willy-nilly with our sanitizing regimes. Again, to be clear, this is not to argue on any level against the need for good hygiene during pandemics, but we need to know that there will be consequences down the road for this.

Summarizing the work of Carl Woese, McFall-Ngai describes how, by the early 1990s, it had become clear that "the earth's biological diversity is far more microbial than ever imagined" (M54) and that "microbes don't just 'rule' the world: they make every life form possible, and they have been doing so since the beginning of evolutionary time" (M59). McFall-Ngai summarizes important arguments about how "bacteria matter not only in themselves but also in relation to other living beings, who depend on them for processes as basic as bodily development" (M59). She spells it out so that even the most nonscientific of readers can clearly understand:

> Bacteria are not only changing the way our guts behave; their metabolic products interact with our entire bodies in complicated ways that we are just beginning to explore. For example, we are finding out that gut bacteria have significant impacts on our brains, affecting the ways we think and feel. (M64)

Citing the work of Yang Wang and Lloyd H. Kaspar, McFall-Ngai contends that "there is growing evidence that the presence or absence of certain microbial strains is linked to depression, anxiety, and autism" (M64). So why in the world is there no media attention to the possible harm that our antiseptic, antibiotic, compulsive sanitizing might be doing to our future? At least part of the answer is quite simply that we do indeed suffer from that branch of ecophobia that Michael Pollan called "germophobia." During the COVID-19 pandemic, his words could not have been timelier.

After SARS, MERS, and COVID-19, a widespread microbiophobia took hold, and hand sanitizers started growing like mold on old bread. Today, as Pollan notes in a discussion about fermentation, "the microbial world is regarded foremost as a mortal threat" (Pollan 2013, 296). The legacy of Louis Pasteur, he explains, "is a century-long war on bacteria, a war in which most of us have volunteered or been enlisted. We deploy our antibiotics and hand sanitizers and deodorants and boiling water and 'pasteurization' and federal regulations to hold off the rot and molds and bacteria and so, we hope, hold off disease and death" (296).[46] Pollan calls it "germophobia" (297), but it is also known as "microbiophobia," "Mysophobia," "verminophobia," "bacillophobia," and "bacteriophobia" – all of them clearly falling under the rubric of ecophobia, which, as I have suggested elsewhere, plays out in many spheres, including the personal hygiene and cosmetics industries (Estok 2009, 208).

What makes Pollan's work so relevant here is that it sidles up to the thin membranes of our most intimate worries, and it pokes at them – and, when they burst, what is "at stake [...] is our whole relationship to nature" (Pollan 2013,

---

[46] Bruno Latour explicitly casts the work of Pasteur in military terms as a war. See Latour 1984.

297). Pollan is relentless – with a nun, no less – in his exploration of what he calls "the erotics of disgust" (360). Sister Noëlla – a post-Pasteurian cheese maker and microbiologist at a Benedictine abbey in Connecticut – reassures Pollan, "Oh, I really like that term" (360). Pollan uses the term because of the ambivalence of our responses to the "various aromas" of our rotting, fermented foods and how they "are often likened to those of the human body in its various parts" (360) – stinky feet, ass sweat, genital musk, and farts (also known as "cutting the cheese"). Pollan goes on to observe that

> the smells we are repressing are of course those of the lower body and the earth, which walking upright allows us to transcend, or at least overlook, in human- ity's age-old top-priority project of putting space between itself and all the other animals. But that project has a cost. The reason those smells so transfix mammals that still walk on four legs is that they contain deeply compelling information, information the high-minded biped is missing. (362)[47]

Those smells contain compelling information about sexual matters, about which foods are edible and which deadly, about how to track food and water, about possible dangers, about fire, and so on; also, that compelling mass of information shows that the body owes everything to what is outside of it and, as Australian feminist philosopher Moira Gatens notes, "is in constant interchange with its environment. The human body is radically open to its surroundings" (Gatens 1996, 110). The porosity of the body, Nancy Tuana explains, "is a hinge through which we are of and in the world" (Tuana 2008, 199). Alaimo calls this porosity "trans-corporeality" and states that "perhaps the most palpable trans-corporeal substance is food, since eating transforms plants and animals into human flesh" (Alaimo 2010, 12). Failing to see this reveals ecophobia and its intersections. One of these intersections, as Pollan engagingly clarifies, has to do with a kind of contempt, fear, and repression of bodily needs and expressions. He quotes French sociologist Pierre Boisard as claiming that food "reminds us of the body, of sensual pleasure, or sexual fulfillment, and of all that is forbidden in it" (Pollan 2013, 363). Startlingly, Pollan then goes on to suggest that the American "government's crackdown on raw-milk cheese is rooted in sexual repression" (363). That crack- down, which is at core microbiophobic and ecophobic, then, as Pollan suggests, intersects with what Greta Gaard has called "erotophobia."[48]

---

[47] Alaimo posits a clearer articulation of the same idea, explaining that "attention to the material transit across bodies and their environments may render it more difficult to seek refuge within fantasies of transcendence or imperviousness" (Alaimo 2010, 16).

[48] In "Toward a Queer Ecofeminism" (1997), Gaard defines "erotophobia" (a fear of eroticism) and how it has always been an environmental issue and a "problem . . . of Western culture, a fear of the erotic so strong that only one form of sexuality is overtly allowed; only in one position; and only in the context of certain legal, religious, and social sanctions" (Gaard 1997, 118). Building on this work, I note in "Theorizing" that one of the manifestations of ecophobia is sometimes

Without question, because various parts of our bodies carry the same bacteria as many foods, the products of those bacteria smell similar: "so it may well be that the allusiveness of a funky cheese to the human body is actually more literal than metaphoric, a matter not so much *this stands for that* as *this is that, too*, in food form" (Pollan 2013, 362–63). We *are* the matter that surrounds us, and our desire to transcend that and to deny materiality and transcorporeality is, as I have said, ecophobic; yet, evolutionary biology favors the fearful, and avoiding rot has clear survival advantages. Avoiding something that will kill you cannot reasonably be called ecophobia, and the sense of disgust has unquestionably had evolutionary roots and functions that have offered survival advantages.

Disgust is a complicated matter, part ideological no doubt but also with genetic roots. It is, as many researchers have shown, an evolutionary response centered on the sense of taste that protects the body from danger or death, and it is not raw or absolute ecophobia. Carroll Izard, for instance, has argued that "in evolution, disgust probably helped motivate organisms to maintain an environment sufficiently sanitary for their health and to prevent them from eating spoiled food and drinking polluted water" (Izard 1977, 337). And, to be clear, an aversion to imagined threats to our survival is not ecophobia, and an aversion to slime (because of its association with disease, rot, and other things that can kill us) is clearly not always ecophobia. Equally clearly, however, slime is not always putrefaction and death. Indeed, slime is the very basis of life itself. We begin as slime, from semen and vaginal secretions, and, millennia before our individual genesis,[49] as primordial slime – hence, perhaps our ambivalent fascination with it. We begin in slime, but slime and rot can have (and have had) mortal consequences.

The body is indeed vulnerable to any of a number of kinds of mortal corruption. It is the body, the sacred house of the human subject, that rot most threatens, and slime is rot's messenger. Slime, to use Kelly Hurley's words, "constitutes a threat to the integrity of the human subject" (Hurley 1996, 35). In the introduction to Aurel Kolnai's landmark work *On Disgust*, Carolyn Korsmeyer and Barry Smith note that the disgusting are "things that are decaying and putrefying, that are contaminated and contaminating, and are thus associated with impurity and threat" (Korsmeyer and Smith 2004, 1–2). Slime is within that category. Robert Wilson explains that slime is central to disgust and that "what is now slime was once something else that

---

a contempt for the body, its functions, and its requirements (Estok 2009, 208). See also note 28 above.

[49] Geology Professor Ross Large has noted that "life remained as little more than a layer of slime for a billion years" (https://theconversation.com/life-on-earth-was-nothing-but-slime-for-a-boring-billion-years-23358).

has degenerated. Slime is disgusting because it is uncertain, a phase in the dissolution of existence" (Wilson 2002, 64). Uncertainty and diversions are threatening: they are the lifeblood of ecophobia.

4 Diversions

4.1 The Agony of Water

When water goes awry and thrashes in an agony of metamorphosis away from its three natural states, it is the stuff of horror – and nowhere is the agony of water more resplendent than in slime. Utterly unpredictable, slime is not subject to control in the way that water is.[50] While "we can never fully direct water's relational reach [, and while it] has a remarkable capacity to resist containments of all kinds" (Chen et al. 2013, 12), we can and do try our very best to control water – and with spectacular results. Water's sometimes random and unpredictable nature fosters both fear and wonder, but slime is more extreme in its evocative range, producing horror on the one hand and puerile wonder on the other. The impulse to control water's apparent randomness and unpredictability has resulted in beautiful and amazingly choreographed displays – such as in the Bellagio Fountains of Las Vegas or the Latona Fountain in the Gardens of Versailles; but there is little taming of slime that inspires aesthetic awe, except, perhaps, in lava lamps. The impulse to control water has resulted in the Hoover Dam and the Three Gorges Dam; harnessing slime does not produce such wonders.[51]

In *Elemental Philosophy*, David Macauley explores how the four elements of ancient philosophy can serve as an organizing set of principles for discussions about contemporary environmental issues, an exploration that both yields many productive insights and perhaps raises questions about whether an interstitial border crosser and intruder such as slime might itself qualify as another element. Macauley speaks of how our "corporeal ties to elemental waters [...] are more than mythic or metaphorical" (Macauley 2010, 45) and notes that these ties are "evident in the fact that our eyes must be bathed frequently in

---

[50] I have often thought that the reason people are so fascinated by fountains has to do with control. Fountains offer the possibility of chaos, the threat of disorder in the very moment that they carefully choreograph every splash and movement of water. Like our childhood fascination with heavy snow and leaf-strewn autumnal streets that temporarily obscure human order, fountains remind us of natural agency (particularly of water), and it is a powerful and potentially deadly agency. Our control over water, it seems, is rarely complete and is often fraught with ambivalence. On a visit to the Three Gorges Dam in 2008, the ambivalence of the visitors (Chinese and foreign) toward the massive structure hailed as a "taming of the Yangtze" was palpable, a taming that cost 200 lives in onsite casualties and displaced more than 1.2 million people.

[51] Parts of this paragraph appear in slightly different form in my "The Slimic Imagination and Elemental Eco-Horror" (Estok 2022, 62). In this article, I examine how slime is central to horror in general and to eco-horror in particular.

salt water, and our body – like the sea – requires a prescribed range of saline in order to sustain life" (45). He goes on to note that there is much about water that remains "random and unpredictable" (48), and it is at this juncture that some comment about slime is appropriate – not only because of our corporeal ties with slime but because of how slime takes "random and unpredictable" to a whole new level.

In spite of yielding to our hand, water still has the *upper* hand: there is more of it than of us (and even the corporeality of "us" is more water than anything), and when unpredictable things such as earthquakes happen, water takes complete control of us. The March 2011 Sendai tsunami is a recent example, but history is dotted with others. Nothing is waterproof. Water carved out the Grand Canyon. It kills countless numbers of people, plants, and animals in storms each year. It freezes and expands and destroys buildings and bridges. It weighs heavily and unpredictably. We have ample reason to fear it as much as to be in awe of it. Yet, it does not epitomize fear in the way that slime does.

Water is a funny element – the only one, as is well-known, that occurs naturally on this planet in the three states of matter (liquid, solid, and gas). In addition to going to these states, water can also go "bad." In VanderMeer's *Annihilation*, it teeters (if water can be said to teeter) between the good and the bad (or at least between what we consider as such). At one point, the pool in the narrator's childhood backyard began to rot, becoming "more and more brackish with algae," but, "by some miracle [...] within months [...] the pool had become a functioning ecosystem" (VanderMeer 2014, 44), replete with local birds, turtles, frogs, and fish. The only thing that the narrator had done to nurture this development was to dump in some fish, most of which died from shock. Nature, having already slimed it up in the pool, did the rest.

Slime is the transgression of all transgressions, of water – the very basis of life. Yet, the transgression of water to slime is a transgression to something that is itself ironically also the very basis of life. As a transgression *par excellence*, slime slips outside of the cultural categories that define the known, the safe, and the normal and falls squarely (as squarely as slime can fall) into the category of what Noël Carroll defines as horror: "what horrifies is that which lies outside cultural categories" (Carroll 1990, 35). Thus, in VanderMeer, the diversions water takes are the stuff of horror.

VanderMeer's is not a dry world, and it is not fear in a handful of dust that he offers; rather, we have eeriness "in the black water with the sun shining at midnight" (VanderMeer 2014, 50). It is an image that looks a lot like the odd stillness and horror of Coleridge's *Rime of the Ancient Mariner*:

Water, water, everywhere,
And all the boards did shrink;
Water, water, everywhere,
Nor any drop to drink.

The very deep did rot: O Christ!
That this should ever be!
Yea, slimy things did crawl with legs
Upon the slimy sea. (Coleridge 1999, ll. 119–26)

In both VanderMeer and Coleridge, water goes awry. In Coleridge, the eerie placidness of the water quickly gives way to sliminess and slimy things crawling; in VanderMeer, as the three remaining women of the expedition in chapter two go down the stairs of the mysterious tunnel/inverted tower, horror is never far away. Not surprisingly, the journey is marked with slime – first with "the trails of snails or slugs" (VanderMeer 2014, 48) and then more definitively with a "slightly viscous [residue], like slime [. . .] about half an inch deep over the steps [. . . and] eight or nine feet wide" (53). If slime signals degeneration, then perhaps it also signals an equally threatening and thwarting of expectations through a kind of re-purposing of material, sometimes with monstrous results.

4.2 Monstrously Divisive Waters

Korean director Bong Joon-ho invokes slime in his 2006 film *The Host* in ways that radically challenge binaristic thinking – in particular, notions about borders and boundaries. Bong is "the first Asian filmmaker to win the Oscar award for Best Director" (Maheshwari 2023)[52] and is Korea's most prolific and successful director. His films have met with tremendous approval among Western audiences while generically refusing the conventions of Western theater. Nam Lee has argued that

> his genre films – whether a crime thriller, monster movie, or science fiction –
> do not give audiences the reassurance offered by their Hollywood counter-
> parts. Rather, his films usually end without a clear sense of resolution, leaving
> the audience puzzled, if not bewildered. The absence of the Hollywood
> "happy ending" constitutes one of the most prominent elements of genre
> subversion in Bong's films. (Lee 2020, 2)

This is significant because Bong divides *and* unites in his films: he establishes filmic conventions that are not Hollywood style (and not Gangnam style) but that mirror its appeal and bring in huge audiences. In many ways indeed, *The Host* is about divisions that unite. These uniting divisions – cultural, ideological, geographical, economic, generational, and gendered – often intersect across the slimic.

---

[52] It was his 2019 film *Parasite* that won this award. The film also won the Academy Award for Best Picture, becoming the first film not in English to do so.

Forcing the audience to confront dividing lines, *The Host* shows the border-lessness of environmental issues in a country riven with divisions. While the Han Gang (Han River) being a poisoned public waterway unites people in a shared threat of vulnerability at the same time that it divides the city into the affluent south (Gangnam) and the less affluent north (Gangbuk),[53] It Is critical also to remember here that vulnerabilities to unsafe water are not shared equally. Water – as Cecilia Chen, Janine MacLeod, and Astrida Neimanis note in their edited collection *Thinking with Water* – is "a matter of concern shared across our differences" (Chen et al. 2013, 7), but those shared differences are not *equally* shared. When water goes awry, it is the communities of the poor that bear the disproportionate burden of suffering.

An important part of this film has to do with notions about dilution (perhaps even reflecting Korean anxieties about cultural dilution threatened by the International Monetary Fund's bailout conditions during East Asian financial crisis, called "the IMF-crisis" in Korea). The dumping scene, then, in addition to raising environmental awareness, is culturally nuanced and committed to resist-ance: there is clearly something different going on in this film than in *Creature from the Black Lagoon*, and rather than exploiting imperialist and colonialist stereotypes, Bong is clearly "writing back" to them. Shortly after the old white man urges the dumping of formaldehyde into the public waterways, we see that the poisons have not diluted and that some people fishing are noticing muta-tions. Soon a monster appears from the river. Water is central in this narrative and becomes both the great equalizer and the great divider. It has the effect in this film of bringing into visibility a world unseen and yet present before our eyes, both disorienting us and, to borrow a description from Melody Jue's description of immersion in water, "shaking up the conditions of interpretation" (Jue 2020, 163). Not confined to the river, however, water is pouring down constantly in the film. The characters are soaked, the monster often slipping on unsure footing, the sense of saturation complete. The watery excess magnifies the horror by invoking slime.

Bong's *The Host* seems to be set during *jangma* (Korea's rainy season), and so the rain is perhaps perfectly plausible; even so, the effect is to create a sense of saturation and sliminess. It is useful to understand saturation in the sense that Melody Jue and Rafico Ruiz use it in their introduction to their edited collection entitled *Saturation: an Elemental Politics*: "while saturation begins with water and watery metaphors," they explain, "it is useful beyond water as a heuristic for thinking through co-present agencies, elements, and phenomena that traverse

---

[53] "Gangnam" is two words: "Gang" from 강, meaning river and "nam" from 남 meaning south. The "buk" in "Gangbuk" is from 북 meaning north. "Gangnam" literally means "south of the river," while "Gangbuk" thus means "north of the river."

ideological systems and physical substances alike" (Jue and Ruiz 2021, 11). In *The Host*, the excess of water leads to a sense of saturation that is complete, and this sense of saturation and excess carries with it a sense of slimic rot, a diversion of water from its proper course and state.

Diversions in *The Host* are both physical and metaphorical – bad liquids being diverted to the wrong place, and ecological systems being de-railed, the latter the consequence of the former. The outcome in *The Host* is a monster that seems irremediably and irrationally evil, bent on the destruction of people and property, heedless of ethics and decency – it does, after all, grab children as they run away. The slimic imbalance that polluted water causes in the film are deadly.

4.3 The Blue Humanities

A focus on planetary water responds to the global concerns of today's ecocatastrophic times. The aims of watery criticism, to adapt a phrase, include both describing the complex workings of water and imagining ways to change our relationships to it. While many neologisms have been proposed, from hydrocriticism to critical ocean studies to ocean history, the sub-disciplinary modes of cultural and literary studies in the early 2020s mostly gather themselves together under the banner of the "blue humanities." (Steve Mentz 2024, 1)[54]

Susanne Wedlich makes the important point that anthropogenic climate change increasingly threatens the balances of our aquatic ecosystems: "Climate change and other catastrophes threaten [these balances], but could also work in slime's favor, ushering in a new era of gooey dominance" (Wedlich 2021, 7). This would not be a good thing. Indeed, central to all meteorological phenomena are the balances of the Earth's oceans, and climate change is shifting the balances and creating positive feedback loops (also known as vicious cycles) between the seas and the skies. When marine systems – what Chen, MacLeod, and Neimanis refer to as the "necessary balance of waters" (Chen et al. 2013, 3) – are disrupted, aquatic and biological effects run deep. One of the problems is that the effects of disrupted balances produce things that evoke fear and hostility toward the environment – an ecophobic response that gels around slime and requires serious immediate attention. The seas are becoming slime, a "nondescript goo" of the jellyfish.[55] The upsliming of the oceans is a global phenomenon, and is not restricted to one place or to jellfish-ization. The "sea snot" in the Sea of Marmara

---

[54] This is the more focused version of his earlier articulation of the blue humanities – under a slightly different name in 2009 – as "the vast and slightly quixotic project of a blue cultural studies, a way of looking at terrestrial literary culture from an offshore perspective, as if we could align ourselves with the watery element" (Mentz 2009, 99). Mentz is often credited with coining the term "blue humanities."

[55] Stacy Alaimo cites this interesting term from www.siphonophores.org/SiphCollecting.php in her "Jellyfish Science, Jellyfish Aesthetics" (Alaimo 2013, 141).

of Turkey is another disturbing example. "Sea snot," Serpil Oppermann explains in her 2023 *Blue Humanities: Storied Waterscapes in the Anthropocene*, is "a mucilage outbreak in the sea" (Oppermann 2023, 20).[56] Triggered by human activities, these outbreaks, Oppermann points out, are devastating for the local marine ecologies. There are, as Mentz states, "multiple forms of planetary water" (Mentz 2024, xii), and while research is moving productively into oceans and seas, it is also gradually moving into fresh waters, bogs, and swamps. As it does so, new areas of slime research will open up, studies of creatures from black lagoons and of biological slimes in brown swamps will surface, and there will develop a virtue in muddy thinking.[57]

It is an open question whether or not UBC marine biologist Daniel Pauly is accurate to suggest "a new name of this new era, the age of slime" instead of the term Anthropocene (Pauly 2010, 61). With the removal of the high end of food chains in global seas, jellyfish are proliferating, and oceans are becoming slime. Thus, Pauly proposes "that [our era] be called 'Myxocene'" (61), the Age of Slime. The horror for Pauly is in the destruction of biotic complexity, the abortion of intricate biotic purposes and aims, and the normalization of bodies of slime (namely jellyfish) floating aimlessly through the annihilated seas. These and other changes that we have wrought "impel research," Stacy Alaimo has argued, "on how gelata affect and are affected by marine environments" (Alaimo 2013, 139). And, to be sure, the research in the Environmental Humanities is increasingly blue.

5 Postscript

The carcass of a Grey Whale that had obviously been at sea for at least a fortnight washed up on Texada Island off the coast of British Columbia in late June of 2021, just in time for the most extreme heatwave in the recorded history of the area. After only a few days in such heat, the carcass had become so slimy that the bald eagles, even with claws that can grab salmon out of whitewater, could not stand long on the body without slipping off. It is the slime to which every human is also slipping as the clock ticks on and on. The stench was profound, and no human would dare to eat of the slime that the birds

---

[56] Oppermann goes on to explain that

> Mucilage is "a gelatinous organic material [...] that can reach great dimensions and cover large areas" (Topçu and Öztürk 2021, 270–71). Released by marine organisms under stress, these "exopolymeric compounds" (2021, 270), or sea snots ("deniz salyası" in Turkish), have impacted mainly the benthic species in the sea of Marmara. (Oppermann 2023, 20)

The devastation is extensive and growing.

[57] The inspiration behind this sentence is Sharon O'Dair's mesmerizing chapter entitled "Muddy Thinking" in the Cohen and Duckert *Elemental Ecocriticism* collection. See O'Dair 2015.

and coastal wolves so readily took as their feasts. That slime would kill us. There are indeed undoubtedly solid evolutionary reasons for myxophobia; yet, myxophobia misunderstands the centrality of slime, its *elemental importance*, to life[58] and in repurposing the products of such life – all life, including human.

Including slime in discussions about elements explicitly recognizes slime, comparable to how trans-friendly bathrooms in Taiwan both recognize the legitimacy of nonbinary people and resist homophobia; not including slime continues both its marginalization as a meaningful matter and the fear and contempt for it that such marginalization evokes. Slime is rarely neutrally adjectival in the way that "pink" or "round" might be. It is an object as well as a description. "An element," Timothy Morton explains, "is a-ness." Thus, "fire is fiery; water is wet; earth is earthiness; space is spacious; and so on" (Morton 2015, 271). Morton makes an important point: adjectives do not have a -nessness; slime does. Slime is slimy, and in its sliminess is danger. It is a dangerous and very unusual element. It sometimes joins, infects, changes, and challenges other elements – sometimes not. The conceptual stakes are high: seeing slime as an element allows discussing it on its own terms rather than as a perversion of something else. The threats slime poses or is imagined to pose fill the pages of literature and history.

Yet, even while recognizing all of this, we must also remember that slime, in and of itself, is a neutral substance. As with all elements, what comes between it and us is important. David Macauley suggests that if we are to change our relationships with the elements (specifically our desire to master and control them), pull out of our current ecocidal trajectory, and ensure sustainable survival for future generations, then it is necessary to begin "to understand the ways we can rein ourselves in and act responsibly" (Macauley 2010, 353). What is at stake here is not simply a set of environmental ethics but an entire worldview. As Timo Müller explained in his ASLE-2021 co-presentation with Moritz Ingwersen, one of the values of "elemental analysis [is that it] helps historicize, diversify, and nuance the concept of material vitality that underlies new materialist approaches" (Ingwersen and Müller 2021, n.pag.). There is no template for understanding these nuances, the ways in which racism, sexism, and classism (along with speciesism and ecophobia) are bound up with our understandings and portrayals of slime. Desired in sexual activity but deplored after; a toy for our young but an embarrassment seeping from our aged; horror

---

[58] When contemplating whales and slime, it is hard not to think of Herman Melville's descriptions of the tubs of sperm that the whalers in the novel collect. Because it has "cooled and crystallized" and "concreted into lumps" (Melville 1988, 372), it has to be massaged and kept liquid in order to retain its commercial value. The descriptions are nothing short of bizarre, the sperm feeling like "fully ripe grapes" (372) with "the smell of spring violets" (372–73). This slime, of elemental importance to life, is harvested through death. Perhaps Goto's clotted masses of slime are an inter-textual response to Melville's.

from the mouth of Mother in the *Alien* franchise but necessary in our own mouths to digest food, slime is complicated. "Slime," Brayton reminds us, "occupies the conceptual space where the human imagination begins to grasp, tentatively and tenuously, the materiality of life itself" (Brayton 2015, 81), but its associations with horror do not, in themselves, prompt political engagement.

Joseph J. Foy, however, maintains differently about eco-horror, arguing that "as a genre, eco-horror attempts to raise mass consciousness about the very real threats that will face humanity if we are not more environmentally cautious" (Foy 2010, 167). For Foy, there are several ways in which "eco-horror films serve as a reminder of the nightmarish future that awaits, and they may advance the type of dialogue that can truly change the cultural conversation" (182): they revitalize "past warnings in an urgent, contemporary context" (168); and their "use of actual environmental issues as the basis of the eco-horror narrative provides a critical look into the current state of global ecology. Together, these combine to raise awareness and begin a dialogue that, when critically examined, can help transform the current political dialogue about domestic and global environmental policy" (171); and they inspire audiences to look at "figures [about] the deaths resulting from climate change" (176). What is missing here is empirical data to support any of these three suppositions.

If eco-horror is simply a subset of the broader horror genre, then how does it warrant Foy's suppositions? Could we not, for instance, make the same claims about any horror film? Could we not propose that the film *Psycho II* (1983) prompts us into action about gender violence, mother/son relations, the nature of psychopathology, and so on; that the film revitalizes discussions about psychiatric and psychological disorders (discussions with a very long history) in an urgent, contemporary context; that the representation of actual psychosocial issues in the film provides a critical look into the current state of mental welfare in America; and that it compels us to look at the numbers about how many people die at the hands of mentally troubled people? Foy tries hard to reconceptualize the horror of eco-horror as somehow exceptional, as politically engaged and ethically astute, but is it?

Certainly it may be, as may be any horror narrative, but there is nothing about eco-horror that makes it intrinsically so. We watch or read eco-horror for the same reasons that we watch or read any horror – namely, for the attraction and repulsion its various slimic traumas offer. Foy is very much alert to something being very different in eco-horror, but the difference is in the element behind the genre, not the genre itself – at least not for the reasons Foy proposes. The element of eco-horror, slime, is political, to be sure, and it is slippery, refusing containment and inhabiting sites of disgust and horror as readily as it does sites of eroticism and joy. It is the harbinger of life and well-being but also of death and disease. Its very elementality is contestable and ambivalent. Indeed, it is precisely its unpredictable and uncontainable agency that makes slime inherently political. It is the agency of slime that produces fear, and it is agency that frequently takes gendered, raced, and classed forms in literature. To address racism, sexism, and classism as they appear in the slimic imagination over millennia means understanding that it is the mutually shared agency imagined as threatening, dangerous, unknowable, and unpredictable that is in the cross-hairs of mediation. This surely is the starting point for any discussion about slimic agency.

Yet, even as we recognize this, it is clear that the discussion here has been lopsided, darker, and less neutral than slime itself, with extended comments on death, ecophobia, monstrosity, and ecohorror. Part of this is simply because "the biological slime we experience is mostly a sign of decay or slime that shows something has gone wrong in our body," but, as Wedlich (a biologist by training) rightly insists, "biological slimes [...] do important and nuanced work [that is] mostly unseen and unnoticed."[59] Biological slime is a fascinating and complex family of substances that are fundamental to life, examples of which would take a much longer and much different volume to explore.

Slime is a radically misunderstood and under-appreciated substance that, as Wedlich explains, has adapted in ways that service our own needs and those of many other (perhaps all) organisms:

> The cervical mucus barrier changes with the menstrual cycle to keep pathogens out and let sperm in only on the fertile days. Mucus molecules in saliva can keep pathogens "in suspended animation," a bit like sleeping beauties: They live on but can't gang up to cause an infection. Snail trails are communication highways that disclose who went where – so that males can follow conspecific females.[60]

Every one of these biological slimes warrants an entire volume, the truth of which is perhaps borne out by Ruth Kassinger's volume on algae (see Kassinger 2020). There is clearly much more work to be done with slime, and Wedlich, it seems, is very accurate to suggest that "hardly anyone knows how fascinating biological slime as a material is."[61]

The elemental turn in the Environmental Humanities revisits old concerns with new perspectives. Expanding elemental discussions to include slime and recognizing that slime is gendered, raced, and classed is necessary to understand our art, ourselves, and how we got these selves into the mess that we are in. We *remain* in a very sexist, racist, and ecophobic world, and this kind of existence is

---

[59] Personal correspondence, April 21, 2024.
[60] Personal correspondence, April 21, 2024.
[61] Personal correspondence, April 21, 2024.

simply not sustainable. Having spiraled further and further away from each other and the world in our move to virtual encounters during the COVID-19 pandemic, we do well now to look at the "perceived relationships between the elements, the body, and the environment [and how] these have exercised an enormous influence on historical beliefs and practices" (Macauley 2010, 71): it is time to think through the mediation of the elements. Macauley explains that mediation matters with the elements: "the elements are socially mediated and constructed through institutional, linguistic, and political practices or beliefs, including those related to marriage, the emotions, war, sex, community structures, and morality" (60). Macauley makes the important point that the English vocabulary "is fraught with links between the elements and the more cultural sphere of language" (60), and he gives examples of how "tropes and metaphors tend to underscore wholeness, cyclicality, and rhythm" (61), many of which – interestingly – slime resists, with few exceptions, implying an imposter quality, a border-crossing nature, and an interloper character absent from the more traditional conception of the elements. We have already seen in VanderMeer's *Annihilation* how slime resists containment. Adam Dickinson's poetic and lyrical *Anatomic* also illustrates well slime's resistance to the tropes and metaphors Macauley describes, and Dickinson's examination of the effects of Anthropocene environments on the human body is one of a very small collection of literary works celebrating slime and the "spectacular and horrifying assemblage" that constitutes "the prosody of [our] metabolism" (Dickinson 2018, 9; 76). Obviously, language is a vital mediator between slime and existence. Sarah Kember and Joanna Zylinska argue powerfully that mediation is a "key trope for understanding and articulating our being in, and becoming with, the technological world, our emergence and ways of intra-acting with it, as well as the acts and processes of temporarily stabilizing the world into media, agents, relations, and networks" (Kember and Zylinska 2012, xv; cf. Jue 2020, 24). Slime is not simply *there*, oozing horror, sexism, and all sorts of prejudices: it is mediated.

Slime appears repeatedly in literature and film, in tales of creatures from black lagoons, and in rimes of ancient mariners. It is part of our food, our collective unconscious, and our intellectual woodshed of rubbish, rot, and decay. It constitutes, enters, exits, and, at times, threatens our bodies and brings us down a notch from our sense of particularity and exceptionalism. Understanding and theorizing about slime is vital not only for disrupting but very likely also for dismantling the ethics of privilege that have defined human relationships with the natural world.

References

Adamson, J., M.M. Evans, and R. Stein, R. 2002. "Introduction: Environmental justice politics, poetics, and pedagogy." In J. Adamson, M.M. Evans, and R. Stein, eds. *The Environmental Justice Reader: Politics, Poetics, and Pedagogy.* Tucson: The University of Arizona Press, pp. 3–14.

Alaimo, S. 2010. *Bodily Natures: Science, Environment, and the Material Self.* Indianapolis: Indiana University Press.

Alaimo, S. 2013. "Jellyfish Science, Jellyfish Aesthetics: Posthuman Reconfigurations of the Sensible." In C. Chen, J. MacLeod, and A. Neimanis, eds. *Thinking with Water.* Montreal: McGill-Queen's University Press, pp. 139–64.

Alaimo, S. 2015. "Elemental Love in the Anthropocene." In J. J. Cohen and L. Duckert, eds. *Elemental Ecocriticism: Thinking with Earth, Air, Water, and Fire.* Minneapolis: University of Minnesota Press, pp. 298–309.

Alberti, F. B. 2016. "A Darke and Vicious Place: Conceptualizing the Vagina How Women's Sex Organs Have Been Understood in Art and in History." *Literary Hub.* https://lithub.com/a-darke-and-vicious-place-conceptualizing-the-vagina/.

Alex, R. K., and S. S. Deborah. 2019. "Ecophobia, Reverential Eco-fear, and Indigenous Worldviews." *ISLE: Interdisciplinary Studies in Literature and Environment* 26(2): 422–29.

Alien 3. 1992. "1991 Teaser Trailer 'The Bitch Is Back'." www.youtube.com/watch?v=S3L3jJyzjFI.

Barnes, H. E. 1990. "Sartre and Sexism." *Philosophy and Literature* 14(2): 340–47.

Bell-Metereau, R. 1985. "Woman: The Other Alien in *Alien*." In J. B. Weedman, ed. *Women Worldwalkers: New Dimensions of Science Fiction and Fantasy.* Lubbock: Texas Tech Press, pp. 9–24.

Born, G. V. R. 1971. *The Born-Einstein Letters: Correspondence between Albert Einstein and Max and Hedwig Born from 1916 to 1955, with Commentaries by Max Born.* Trans. I. Newton-John. London: Macmillan.

Boyarin, D. 1995. "Homotopia: The Feminized Jewish Man and the Lives of Women in Late Antiquity." *Differences: A Journal of Feminist Cultural Studies* 7(2): 41–81.

Branch, M., and S. O'Grady. 1994. "Defining Ecocritical Theory: Introduction." *ASLE: Association for the Study of Literature and Environment.* www.asle.org/wp-content/uploads/ASLE_Primer_DefiningEcocrit.pdf.

Brayton, D. 2015. "Shakespeare and Slime: Notes and the Anthropocene." In J. Munroe, E. J. Geisweidt, and L. Bruckner, eds. *Ecological Approaches to Early Modern English Texts: A Field Guide to Reading and Teaching.* Farnham: Ashgate, pp. 81–90.

Brontë, C. 1971. *Jane Eyre*, edited by R. J. Dunn. New York: Norton.

Butler, J. 1993. *Bodies that Matter: On the Discursive Limits of "Sex."* New York: Routledge.

Camara, A. 2014. "Abominable Transformations: Becoming-Fungus in Arthur Machen's 'The Hill of Dreams'." *Gothic Studies* 16(1): 9–23.

Carroll, N. 1990. *The Philosophy of Horror, or Paradoxes of the Heart.* New York: Routledge.

Chakrabarty, D. 2019. "The Climate of History: Four Theses." *Critical Inquiry* 35(2): 197–222.

Chen, M. Y. 2012. *Animacies: Biopolitics, Racial Mattering, and Queer Affect.* Durham: Duke University Press.

Chen, C., J. MacLeod, and A. Neimanis. 2013. "Introduction: Toward a Hydrological Turn." In C. Chen, J. MacLeod, and A. Neimanis, eds. *Thinking with Water.* Montreal: McGill-Queen's University Press, pp. 3–22.

Chiari, S. 2019. *Shakespeare's Representation of Weather, Climate and Environment: The Early Modern "Fated Sky."* Edinburgh: Edinburgh University Press.

Chow, J. 2023. *The Queerness of Water: Troubled Ecologies in the Eighteenth Century.* Charlottesville: University of Virginia Press.

Cohen, J. J. and L. Duckert. 2015. "Introduction: Eleven Principles of the Elements." In J. J. Cohen and L. Duckert, eds. *Elemental Ecocriticism: Thinking with Earth, Air, Water, and Fire.* Minneapolis: University of Minnesota Press, pp. 1–26.

Coleridge, S. T. 1999. *The Rime of the Ancient Mariner: Case Studies in Contemporary Criticism*, edited by P. H. Fry. Boston: Bedford/St. Martin's.

Collins, M. and C. Pierce. 1976. "Holes and Slime: Sexism in Sartre's Psychoanalysis." In C. C. Gould and M. W. Wartofsky, eds. *Women and Philosophy: Toward a Theory of Liberation.* New York: Putnam's Sons, pp. 112–27.

Coole, D., and S. Frost. 2010. "Introducing the New Materialisms." In D. Coole and S. Frost. eds. *New Materialisms: Ontology, Agency, and Politics.* Durham: Duke University Press, pp. 1–43.

Creed, B. 1993. *The Monstrous-Feminine: Film, Feminism, Psychoanalysis.* London: Routledge.

Davis, M. 2000. "'What's the Story Mother?': Abjection and Anti-Feminism in *Alien* and *Aliens*." *Gothic Studies* 2(2): 245–56.

Dickens, C. 1980. *Great Expectations*, edited by R. D. McMaster. Toronto: Gage.

Dickinson, A. 2018. *Anatomic*. Toronto: Coach House.

Dillard, A. 1985. *Pilgrim at Tinker Creek*. New York: Harper Perennial.

Douglas, M. 1984. *Purity and Danger: An Analysis of the Concepts of Pollution and Taboo*. New York: Routledge.

Doherty, T. 2015. "Gender, Genre, and the Aliens Trilogy." In K. Grant, ed. *The Dread of Difference Gender and the Horror Film*. Austin: University of Texas Press, pp. 209–27.

Ehrenfeld, D. 1981. *The Arrogance of Humanism*. Oxford: Oxford University Press.

Empson, W. 1964. "The Ancient Mariner." *Critical Quarterly* 6(4): 298–319. https://doi.org/10.1111/criq.1964.6.issue-4.

Estok, S. C. 2009. "Theorizing in a Space of Ambivalent Openness: Ecocriticism and Ecophobia." *Interdisciplinary Studies in Literature and Environment* 16(2): 203–25.

Estok, S. C. 2018. *The Ecophobia Hypothesis*. New York: Routledge.

Estok, S. C. 2019. "The Environmental Imagination in the Slime of the Ancient Mariner." *ANQ: A Quarterly Journal of Short Articles, Notes and Reviews* 34(2): 135–38.

Estok, S. C. 2020. "Afterword: New Horizons in Materiality and Literature." *Neohelicon: Acta Comparationis Litterarum Universarum* 47: 587–94.

Estok, S. C. 2022. "The Slimic Imagination and Elemental Eco-Horror," *ZAA: Zeitschrift für Anglistik und Amerikanistik* 70(1): 59–74.

Estok, S. C. 2023a. "Pulped and Reduced, Dried Out and Flattened: The Horrors of Aborted Agency in 'The Yellow Wallpaper'." *Studies in American Fiction* 50(1–2): 75–96.

Estok, S. C. 2023b. "Slime, Gender, and Environment: Misogyny's Slimic Entanglements with Ecophobia." *ANQ: A Quarterly Journal of Short Articles, Notes and Reviews*. https://doi.org/10.1080/0895769X.2023.2258179.

Flores, T. 2021. "Can Playing with Slime Actually Benefit Your Mental Health?" *The Huffington Post*. www.huffpost.com/entry/slime-mental-health_1_61607c96e4b0cc44c50c70d1.

Foley, S. F., Gronenborn, D., and Andreae, M. O et al. 2013. "The Palaeoanthropocene – The Beginnings of Anthropogenic Environmental Change." *Anthropocene* 3: 83–88. www.sciencedirect.com/science/article/abs/pii/S2213305413000404.

Foy, J. J. 2010. "It Came from Planet Earth: Eco-Horror and the Politics of Post-Environmentalism in *The Happening*." In T. M. Dale and J. J. Foy, eds. *Homer Simpson Marches on Washington: Dissent Through American Popular Culture*. Lexington: University Press of Kentucky, pp. 167–88.

Fulford, T. 2006. "Slavery and Superstition in the Supernatural Poems." In L. Newlyun, ed. *The Cambridge Companion to Coleridge*. Cambridge: Cambridge University Press, pp. 45–58.

Gaard, G. 1997. "Toward a Queer Ecofeminism." *Hypatia* 12(1): 114–37.

Gaard, G. 2010. "New Directions for Ecofeminism: Toward a More Feminist Ecocriticism." *ISLE: Interdisciplinary Studies in Literature and Environment* 17(4): 643–65.

Gaard, G. 2011. "Green, Pink, and Lavender: Banishing Ecophobia Through Queer Ecologies." *Ethics and Environment* 16(2): 155–226.

Gatens, M. 1996. *Imaginary Bodies: Ethics, Power, and Corporeality*. New York: Routledge.

Gilman, C. P. 1995. "The Yellow Wallpaper." In M. Ford and J. Ford, eds. *Imagining Worlds*. New York: McGraw Hill, pp. 600–12.

Goto, H. 2022. "And the Moon Spun Round Like a Top." In D. Zomparelli and D. Ly, eds. *Queer Little Nightmares: An Anthology of Monstrous Fiction and Poetry*. Vancouver: Arsenal Press, pp. 109–36.

Harman, G. 2012. *Weird Realism: Lovecraft and Philosophy*. Winchester: Zero Books.

Heckman, S. 2010. *The Material of Knowledge: Feminist Disclosures*. Bloomington: Indiana University Press.

Houellebecq, M. 2005. *H. P. Lovecraft: Against the World, against Life*. San Francisco: Believer Magazine.

Hurley, K. 1996. *The Gothic Body: Sexuality, Materialism, and Degeneration at the fin de siècle*. Cambridge: Cambridge University Press.

Ingwersen, M., and T. Müller. 2021."Mobilizing the Elemental Turn in Contemporary Ecocriticism." *YouTube Video*, Conference Paper Recording, *ASLE 2021: Emergence/y*. www.youtube.com/watch?v=QVUMPkLeojg.

Ingwersen, M., and T. Müller. 2022. "The Aesthetics and Politics of Elemental Agency." *Zeitschrift für Anglistik und Amerikanistik* 70(1): 3–22.

Iovino, S. 2013. "Toxic Epiphanies: Dioxin, Power, and Gendered Bodies in Laura Conti's Narratives on Seveso." In G. Gaard, S. C. Estok, and S. Oppermann, eds. *International Perspectives on Feminist Ecocriticism*. New York: Routledge, pp. 37–55.

Iovino, S., and S. Oppermann. 2014. "Introduction: Stories Come to Matter." In S. Iovino and S. Oppermann, eds. *Material Ecocriticism*. Bloomington: Indiana University Press, pp. 1–17.

Izard, C. E. 1977. *Human Emotions*. New York: Springer.

Johnson, S. 2004. *Emergence: The Connected Lives of Ants, Brains, Cities, and Software*. New York: Scribner.

Jue, M. 2020. *Wild Blue Media: Thinking Through Seawater*. Durham: Duke University Press.

Jue, M., and R. Ruiz. 2021. "Thinking with Saturation Beyond Water: Thresholds, Phase Change, and the Precipitate." In M. Jue and R. Ruiz, eds. *Saturation: An Elemental Politics*. Durham: Duke University Press, pp. 1–26.

Kassinger, R. 2020. *Slime: How Algae Created Us, Plague Us, and Just Might Save Us*. Boston: Houghton Mifflin Harcourt.

Kavanagh, J. H. 1990. "Feminism, Humanism and Science in *Alien*." In A. Kuhn, ed. *Alien Zone Cultural Theory and Contemporary Science Fiction Cinema*. New York: Verso, pp. 73–81.

Kember, S., and J. Zylinska. 2012. *Life after New Media: Mediation as Vital Process*. Cambridge, MA: MIT Press.

Kniss, A. 2023. "In the Earth and Gaia: A Review Cluster." *Gothic Nature: New Directions in EcoHorror and the EcoGothic* 4: 248–253. https://gothicnature journal.com/wp-content/uploads/2023/05/GothicNatureIssueIV.pdf.

Koch, E. 2023. "Book Review: Aliya Whiteley, *The Secret Life of Fungi: Discoveries from a Hidden World*." *Gothic Nature: New Directions in EcoH"orror and the EcoGothic* 4: 278–81. https://gothicnaturejournal.com/wp-content/uploads/2023/05/GothicNatureIssueIV.pdf.

Korsmeyer, C. and B. Smith. 2004. "Visceral Values: Aurel Kolnai on Disgust." In A. Kolnai, with B. Smith and C. Korsmeyer, eds. *On Disgust*. Chicago: Open Court, pp. 1–25.

Kristeva, J. 1982. *Powers of Horror: An Essay on Abjection*. Trans. L. S. Roudiez. New York: Columbia University Press.

Kroeber, K. 1957. "The Rime of the Ancient Mariner as Stylized Epic." In J. Larsen, ed. *Transactions of the Wisconsin Academy of Sciences, Arts and Letters* XLVI. Madison: Wisconsin Academy of Sciences, Arts and Letters, pp. 179–87.

Kroeber, K. 1994. *Ecological Literary Criticism: Romantic Imagining and the Biology of Mind*. New York: Columbia University Press.

Large, R. 2014. "Life on Earth Was Nothing but Slime for a 'Boring Billion' Years." *The Conversation* https://theconversation.com/life-on-earth-was-nothing-but-slime-for-a-boring-billion-years-23358.

Latour, B. 1984. *The Pasteurization of France*. Trans. A. Sheridan and J. Law. Cambridge, MA: Cambridge University Press.

Latour, B. 2004. *Politics of Nature: How to Bring the Sciences into Democracy*. Trans. C. Porter. Cambridge: Harvard University Press.

Lee, N. 2020. *The Films of Bong Joon Ho*. New Brunswick, NJ: Rutgers University Press.

Lindes, P. 2020. "Intelligence and Agency." *Journal of Artificial General Intelligence* 11(1): 1–3.

Lingis, A. 2000. *Dangerous Emotions*. Berkeley: University of California Press.

Macauley, D. 2010. *Elemental Philosophy: Earth, Air, Fire, and Water as Environmental Ideas*. New York: State University of New York Press.

Machen, A. 2018. "'The Great God Pan' and 'The Three Imposters'" In A. Worth, ed. *The Great God Pan and Other Horror Stories*. Oxford: Oxford University Press, pp. 9–54; 79–196.

Mackey, A. 2023. "In the Earth and Gaia: A Review Cluster." *Gothic Nature: New Directions in EcoHorror and the EcoGothic* 4: 253–61. https://gothicnaturejournal.com/wp-content/uploads/2023/05/GothicNatureIssueIV.pdf.

Maheshwari, D. 2023. "Korean Films at the Oscars: Nominations and Wins with Parasite, Minari, and More." *Pinkvialla*. www.pinkvilla.com/entertainment/korean-films-at-the-oscars-nominations-and-wins-with-parasite-minari-and-more-1207092#:~:text=By%20winning%20the%20Best%20Picture,Oscar%20award%20for%20Best%20Director.

Marchesini, R. 2021. *The Virus Paradigm: A Planetary Ecology of the Mind*. Trans. S. De Sanctis. Cambridge: Cambridge University Press.

Martel, Y. 2001. *The Life of Pi*. Toronto: Vintage.

McFall-Ngai, M. 2017. "Noticing Microbial Worlds: The Postmodern Synthesis in Biology." In E. Gan, A. Tsing, H. Swanson, and N. Bubandt, eds. *Arts of Living on a Damaged Planet*. Minneapolis: University of Minnesota Press, pp. M51–M69.

Melville, H. 1988. *Moby Dick*. Ed. with an Introduction and Notes by T. Tanner. Oxford: Oxford University Press.

Mentz, S. 2009. *At the Bottom of Shakespeare's Ocean*. New York: Continuum.

Mentz, S. 2024. *An Introduction to the Blue Humanities*. New York: Routledge.

Merrigan, T. W. 2014. "The 8 Books You Need to Know This Month." *GQ* 21 www.gq.com/gallery/the-best-books-for-february-2014#slide=2.

Michael, M. 2016. "Lovecraft Was Very Racist: Six Passages to That Effect." *Pudding Shot*. https://puddingshot.wordpress.com/2016/07/31/lovecraft-was-very-racist-six-passages-to-that-effect/.

Miller, W. I. 1997. *The Anatomy of Disgust*. Cambridge, MA: Harvard University Press.

Misra, A. 2023. "The Science behind Zombie Viruses and Infections: The Concept of Infection Is Rooted in Scientific Truth." *Cleveland Clinic: Health Essentials*. https://health.clevelandclinic.org/zombie-virus.

Morton, T. 2007. *Ecology without Nature: Rethinking Environmental Aesthetics*. Cambridge: Harvard University Press.

Morton, T. 2013. *Hyperobjects: Philosophy and Ecology after the End of the World*. Minneapolis: University of Minnesota Press.

Morton, T. 2015. "Elementality." In J. J. Cohen and L. Duckert, eds. *Elemental Ecocriticism: Thinking with Earth, Air, Water, and Fire*. Minnesota: University of Minnesota Press, pp. 271–85.

Mui, C. 1990. "Sartre's Sexism Reconsidered." *Auslcgung* 16(1): 31–41.

Myers, J. 2023. "The Madness of Mold: Ecogothic in Nathaniel Hawthorne's *the House of the Seven Gables*." *Studies in American Fiction* 50(1–2): 11–30.

Neimanis, A. 2017. *Bodies of Water: Posthuman Feminist Phenomenology*. London: Bloomsbury.

Newton, J. 1990. "Feminism and Anxiety in *Alien*." In A. Kuhn, ed. *Alien Zone: Cultural Theory and Contemporary Science Fiction*. New York: Verso, pp. 82–90.

Nixon, R. 2011. *Slow Violence and the Environmentalism of the Poor*. Boston: Harvard University Press.

Nussbaum, M. 2018. "The Roots of Male Rage, on Show at the Kavanaugh Hearing." *The Washington Post*. www.washingtonpost.com/news/democ racy-post/wp/2018/09/29/the-roots-of-male-rage-on-show-at-the-kava naugh-hearing/.

O'Dair, S. 2015. "Muddy Thinking." In J. J. Cohen and L. Duckert, eds. *Elemental Ecocriticism: Thinking with Earth, Air, Water, and Fire*. Minneapolis: University of Minnesota Press, pp. 134–57.

Oakley-Brown, L. 2024. *Shakespeare on the Ecological Surface*. New York: Routledge.

Oken, L. 1847/2015. *Elements of Physiophilosophy*, Translated from German by Alfred Tulk. London: The Ray Society. www.gutenberg.org/cache/epub/ 49196/pg49196-images.html.

Olsen, N. 2023. "Foods to Eat for Better Sex." *Medical News Today*. www .medicalnewstoday.com/articles/322779#circulation-and-stamina.

Oppermann, S. 2017. "Compost." In J. J. Cohen and L. Duckert, eds. *Veer Ecology: A Companion for Environmental Thinking*. Minnesota: University of Minnesota Press, pp. 136–50.

Oppermann, S. 2023. *Blue Humanities: Storied Waterscapes in the Anthropocene*. Cambridge: Cambridge University Press.

Paglia, C. 1990. *Sexual Personae: Art and Decadence from Nefertiti to Emily Dickinson*. New York: Vintage.

Paster, G. K. 1993. *The Body Embarrassed: Drama and the Disciplines of Shame in Early Modern England*. Ithaka: Cornell University Press.

Pastore, C. 2019. "A Thousand, Thousand Slimy Things: A Natural History of the Sea from the Bottom Up." A lecture given at Trinity College, Dublin.

https://soundcloud.com/tlrhub/a-thousand-thousand-slimy-things-a-natural-history-of-the-sea-from-the-bottom-up.

Pauly, D. 2010. *Five Easy Pieces: The Impact of Fisheries on Marine Ecosystems*, Reprint Ed. Washington, DC: Island Press.

Peters, J. D. 2015. *The Marvelous Clouds: Toward a Philosophy of Elemental Media*. Chicago: University of Chicago Press.

Pitt, S. 2019. "Snail Slime: The Science behind Molluscs as Medicine." *The Conversation*. https://theconversation.com/snail-slime-the-science-behind-molluscs-as-medicine-125156.

Pollan, M. 2013. *Cooked: A Natural History of Transformation*. New York: Penguin.

Powers, R. 2018. *The Overstory*. London: Penguin.

Read, S. 2013. *Menstruation and the Female Body in Early Modern England*. Basingstoke: Palgrave.

Roth, P. 2010. *Nemesis*. New York: Vintage.

Rozelle, L. 2016. *Zombiescapes and Phantom Zones: Ecocriticism and the Liminal from the Invisible Man to the Walking Dead*. Tuscaloosa: University of Alabama Press.

Rucker, P. 2015. "Trump Says Fox's Megyn Kelly Had 'Blood Coming Out of Her Wherever.'" *The Washington Post* www.washingtonpost.com/news/post-politics/wp/2015/08/07/trump-says-foxs-megyn-kelly-had-blood-coming-out-of-her-wherever/.

Rushing, J. H. 1989. "Evolution of 'The New Frontier' in *Alien* and *Aliens*: Patriarchal Co-Optation of the Feminine Archetype." *The Quarterly Journal of Speech* 75(1): 1–24.

Sartre, J.-P. 1966. *Being and Nothingness: A Phenomenological Essay on Ontology*, trans. H. E. Barnes. New York: First Pocket Books.

Shakespeare, W. 1997a. *King Lear*. In G. Blakemore Evans, J. J. M. Tobin, F., and Kermode, eds. *The Riverside Shakespeare*, *2nd Ed*. Boston: Houghton Mifflin, pp. 1297–354.

Shakespeare, W. 1997b. *Titus Andronicus*. In G. Blakemore Evans, J. J. M. Tobin, F., and Kermode, eds. *The Riverside Shakespeare*, *2nd Ed*. Boston: Houghton Mifflin, pp. 1065–100.

Shakespeare, W. 1997c. "Sonnet 153." In G. Blakemore Evans, J. J. M. Tobin, F., and Kermode, eds. *The Riverside Shakespeare*, *2nd Ed*. Boston: Houghton Mifflin, p. 1871.

Shakespeare, W. 1997d. *Hamlet*. In G. Blakemore Evans, J. J. M. Tobin, F., and Kermode, eds. *The Riverside Shakespeare*, *2nd Ed*. Boston: Houghton Mifflin, pp. 1183–245.

Sharp, Jane. 1999. *The Midwives Book; or, the Whole Art of Midwifry Discovered*. Ed. Elaine Hobby. Oxford: Oxford University Press.

Sheldrake, M. 2020. *Entangled Life: How Fungi Make Our Worlds, Change Our Minds, and Shape Our Futures*. New York: Random House.

Sivils, M. W. 2023. "Introduction: The Proliferation of the Ecogothic." *Studies in American Fiction* 50(1–2): 1–9.

Skeat, W. W. 1980. *A Concise Etymological Dictionary of the English Language*. New York: Perigee.

"Slime: Can it be environmentally friendly?" 2018. *CBBC Newsround* www .bbc.co.uk/newsround/45560860.

Sokal, A. 1996. "A Physicist Experiments with Cultural Studies." *Lingua Franca* https://web.archive.org/web/20071005011354/http://linguafranca .mirror.theinfo.org/9605/sokal.html.

Stevenson, R. L. 2003. *The Strange Case of Dr. Jekyll and Mr. Hyde*. New York: Signet.

Swift, J. 1960. *Gulliver's Travels and Other Writings*, edited by L. A. Landa. Boston: Houghton Mifflin.

Thacker, E. 2011. *In the Dust of this Planet: Horror of Philosophy. Vol. 1*. Hampshire: Zero Books.

Tidwell, C. 2023. "In the Earth and Gaia: A Review Cluster". *Gothic Nature: New Directions in EcoHorror and the EcoGothic* 4: 246–48. https://gothicna turejournal.com/wp-content/uploads/2023/05/GothicNatureIssueIV.pdf.

Topçu, N. E., and B. Öztürk. 2021. "The Impact of the Massive Mucilage Outbreak in the Sea of Marmara on Gorgonians of Prince Islands: A Qualitative Assessment." *Black Sea/Mediterranean Environment* 27(2): 270–78. https://blackmeditjournal.org/volumes-archive/vol-27-2021/vol-27-2021-no-2/the-impact-of-the-massive-mucilage-outbreak-in-the-sea-ofmarmara-on-gorgonians-of-prince-islands-a-qualitative-assessment/.

Tsing, A. L. 2015. *The Mushroom at the End of the World: On the Possibility of Life in Capitalist Ruins*. Princeton: Princeton University Press.

Tuana, N. 2008. "Viscous Porosity: Witnessing Katrina." In S. Alaimo and S. Hekman, eds. *Material Feminisms*. Indianaplois: Indiana University Press, pp. 188–213.

VanderMeer, J. 2014. *Annihilation*. New York: Farrar, Straus and Giroux.

Vaughn, T. 1995. "Voices of Sexual Distortion: Rape, Birth, and Self-Annihilation Metaphors in the Alien Trilogy." *Quarterly Journal of Speech* 81(4): 423–35.

Wald, P. 2008. *Contagious: Cultures, Carriers, and the Outbreak Narrative*. Durham: Duke University Press.

Wang, Y., and L. H. Kaspar. 2014. "The Role of the Microbiome in Central Nervous System Disorders." *Brain, Behavior, and Immunity* 38: 1–12. https://doi.org/10.1016/j.bbi.2013.12.015.

Wedlich, S. 2021. *Slime: A Natural History*. London: Granta.

Weisman, A. 2007. *The World without Us*. New York: Picador.

Weiss, A. 1992. *Vampires and Violets: Lesbians in Film*. New York: Penguin.

Whitmarsh, P. 2023. "'We Live below Sea Level': Layered Ecologies and Regional Gothic in Karen Russell's *Swamplandia!*" *Studies in American Fiction* 50(1–2): 143–64.

Wilson, R. R. 2002. *The Hydra's Tale: Imagining Disgust*. Edmonton: University of Alberta Press.

Woodard, B. 2012. *Slime Dynamics*. Hampshire: Zero Books.

Woolbright, L. 2023. "The Megamycete at the End of the World: Resident Evil: Village and Gothic Ecophobia." *Gothic Nature: New Directions in EcoHorror and the EcoGothic* 4: 240–43. https://gothicnaturejournal.com/wp-content/uploads/2023/05/GothicNatureIssueIV.pdf.

Wright, L. 2015. *The Vegan Studies Project: Food, Animals, and Gender in the Age of Terror*. Athens: University of Georgia Press.

Yong, E. 2016. *I Contain Multitudes: The Microbes within Us and a Grander View of Life*. New York: HarperCollins.

Acknowledgments

It takes a village to write a book, and a solid pandemic doesn't hurt either. Most of this book morphed and oozed into shape while COVID-19 raged on. During that the same time, the sale of children's slime kits soared, suggesting that such substances somehow ease stress. Both kids and adults, meanwhile, were squirting sanitizer on their hands and thus smothering potential pathogens to death in slime. With its dual offer both of salvation from stress and survival over mortality, things were looking up for slime. If you went into a spring-cleaning fit during one of the lockdowns, however, and discovered a long-forgotten squash dripping its discontents at the back reaches of the fridge, then the reality of slime's ambivalence may have hit home. It did for me. This book is in part a pandemic baby.

I am grateful to several people for allowing me to test my ideas at their institutions: Serpil Oppermann at Cappadocia University; Chun Yui Shing and Emily Zong at Hong Kong Baptist University; Kim Jonggab at Konkuk University; Kim Won-Chung at Sungkyunkwan University; Curtis Whitaker (Idaho State University) for having me on the panel at the 2019 ASLE conference at the University of California, Davis; József Pál at the University of Szeged; Péter Hajdu at Shenzhen University; and Cao Shunqing at Sichuan University.

Many people listened to, commented on, or read parts of this book. I am especially grateful to Susanne Wedlich, Matthew Wynn Sivils, Dan Brayton, I-min (Peter) Huang, Iris Ralph, Scott Slovic, David Suzuki, Christopher Pastore, Timothy Morton, Peina Zhuang, Greta Gaard, Ursula Heise, and Narie Jung. I also wish to thank Jonathan White and Susan Oliver for having me and my teenagers at their Oast House flat in Cambridge in August 2023 and for the invigorating conversations we had over dinner (and over a solid single malt) during our London visit.

It would be very remiss of me not to mention the staff of the Sungkyunkwan University Library for their dazzling efficiency, kindness, and patience with my "EXTREMELY URGENT" emails. The staff always got articles and books either on loan or for keeps from sellers and libraries within Korea and from abroad with absolutely implausible speed. I also want to thank Sungkyunkwan University for its unwavering support and promotion of my research.

I am deeply grateful to the Cambridge Elements Series editors Serenella Iovino, Timo Maran, and Louise Westling for the extraordinary quality of titles that they have hosted, for the positive and constructive atmosphere that they foster, and for the brilliance of their suggestions and comments. For their meticulous and insightful comments, the anonymous reviewers helped make this book better and fuller than it was, and I thank them. I also wish to express my gratitude to Ray Ryan at Cambridge University Press and to Sowmya Singaravelu and Narmadha Nedounsejiane at Integra Software Services.

Bits and chunks of this Element appeared in earlier forms in *Postmedieval: a Journal of Medieval Cultural Studies*; *Neohelicon. Acta comparationis litterarum universarum*; *ANQ: A Quarterly Journal of Short Articles, Notes, and Reviews*; *Cultura. International Journal of Philosophy of Culture and Axiology*; *ISLE: Interdisciplinary Studies in Literature and Environment*; *ELN: English Language Notes, Zeitschrift für Anglistik und Amerikanistik* (*ZAA: a quarterly of language, literature and culture*); and *Configurations: a Journal of Literature, Science, and Technology.*

Finally, I want to thank my teenage children, Jonathan and Sophia (for saying "okay" whenever I asked "wanna hear what Dad's working on these days?"), and their mother Cho Yeon-hee, who does all of the practical stuff while I'm away in Seoul. For more than half of the twenty years that we have been married, Yeon-hee has been doing this heroic and taxing work seven months of the year while I am in Seoul. It is a debt for which I can only say "정말 고마워요."

To the memory of my father
לעילוי נשמת אבי ע״ה

Cambridge Elements ≡

Environmental Humanities

Louise Westling
University of Oregon

Louise Westling is an American scholar of literature and environmental humanities who was a founding member of the Association for the Study of Literature and Environment and its President in 1998. She has been active in the international movement for environmental cultural studies, teaching and writing on landscape imagery in literature, critical animal studies, biosemiotics, phenomenology, and deep history.

Serenella Iovino
University of North Carolina at Chapel Hill

Serenella Iovino is Professor of Italian Studies and Environmental Humanities at the University of North Carolina at Chapel Hill. She has written on a wide range of topics, including environmental ethics and ecocritical theory, bioregionalism and landscape studies, ecofeminism and posthumanism, comparative literature, eco-art, and the Anthropocene.

Timo Maran
University of Tartu

Timo Maran is an Estonian semiotician and poet. Maran is Professor of Ecosemiotics and Environmental Humanities and Head of the Department of Semiotics at the University of Tartu. His research interests are semiotic relations of nature and culture, Estonian nature writing, zoosemiotics and species conservation, and semiotics of biological mimicry.

About the Series

The environmental humanities is a new transdisciplinary complex of approaches to the embeddedness of human life and culture in all the dynamics that characterize the life of the planet. These approaches reexamine our species' history in light of the intensifying awareness of drastic climate change and ongoing mass extinction. To engage this reality, Cambridge Elements in Environmental Humanities builds on the idea of a more hybrid and participatory mode of research and debate, connecting critical and creative fields.

Cambridge Elements ≡

Environmental Humanities

Elements in the Series

Printed in the United States
by Baker & Taylor Publisher Services